How to use your Letts Motor Tour Guide

The best way to see Britain is, for most people, by car. This Tour Guide has been specially designed to lead you—the motorist—to all that is best in its chosen area.

The Lake District, The Pennines and Yorkshire Dales

This series of tours explores *three* beautiful and well-loved areas: the Yorkshire Dales, varied and pleasant valleys; the Lake District, for many the loveliest and most satisfying part of England; and the wild Pennine moorlands, with grand stretches of escarpment, reaching north to the historic Hadrian's Wall.

Well-known places of interest are visited; so, too, are many out-of-the-way and lesser-known spots. Places visited on these tours include favoured holiday spas, lakeside resorts, charming villages, fascinating old market towns, impressive medieval ruins, and caves and waterfalls.

The Tours

There are ten motor tours in this Guide and each tour covers about a hundred miles. If you wish to visit and explore all the places mentioned, you may find that a single tour will provide two or more good days' motoring. All the tours are circular, and so you can start and finish a route at any other point you may choose. The book is yours to use in your own way.

The Maps

The maps (one for each tour and a larger one for the whole area) have been specially designed to show clearly all the information you will need—without being unduly technical. Readers who lack expertise in map-reading will have no difficulty in following the directions and the route. The main approach roads to the tours are also indicated.

continued

Reference Books

For those who wish to use more detailed maps, Sheet 9 of the Ordnance Survey quarter-inch maps covers most of the Pennines and the Yorkshire Dales, while Sheet 8 covers the Lake District.

Particulars are given in the tours of the days and times of opening for houses, castles and museums, and these are correct at the time of going to press. The most recent information can be obtained from *Historic Houses, Castles and Gardens in Great Britain*, which is published annually in February. Details regarding museums and art galleries are given in *Museums and Galleries in Great Britain*, published yearly in July.

Particulars of hotels, restaurants and inns are given in the annual reference guide, *Hotels and Restaurants in Britain*, published by the British Travel Association. An annual selective and critical guide to eating places is Raymond Postgate's *Good Food Guide*, and a more extensive annual critical guide to hotels, restaurants, pubs and inns is written by Egon Ronay. All the above books may be purchased from any bookseller, or referred to at a library.

Letts Motor Tour Guides

Printed and Published by
Charles Letts & Company Limited
London, Edinburgh & New York
Head Office:
Diary House, Borough Road, London, S.E.1

Publishing Consultant: Lionel Leventhal

Cover Artist: Kenneth Farnhill

Maps: Jack Parker

The Lake District, The Pennines and Yorkshire Dales
by F. R. Banks
first published 1969

Contents

Maps

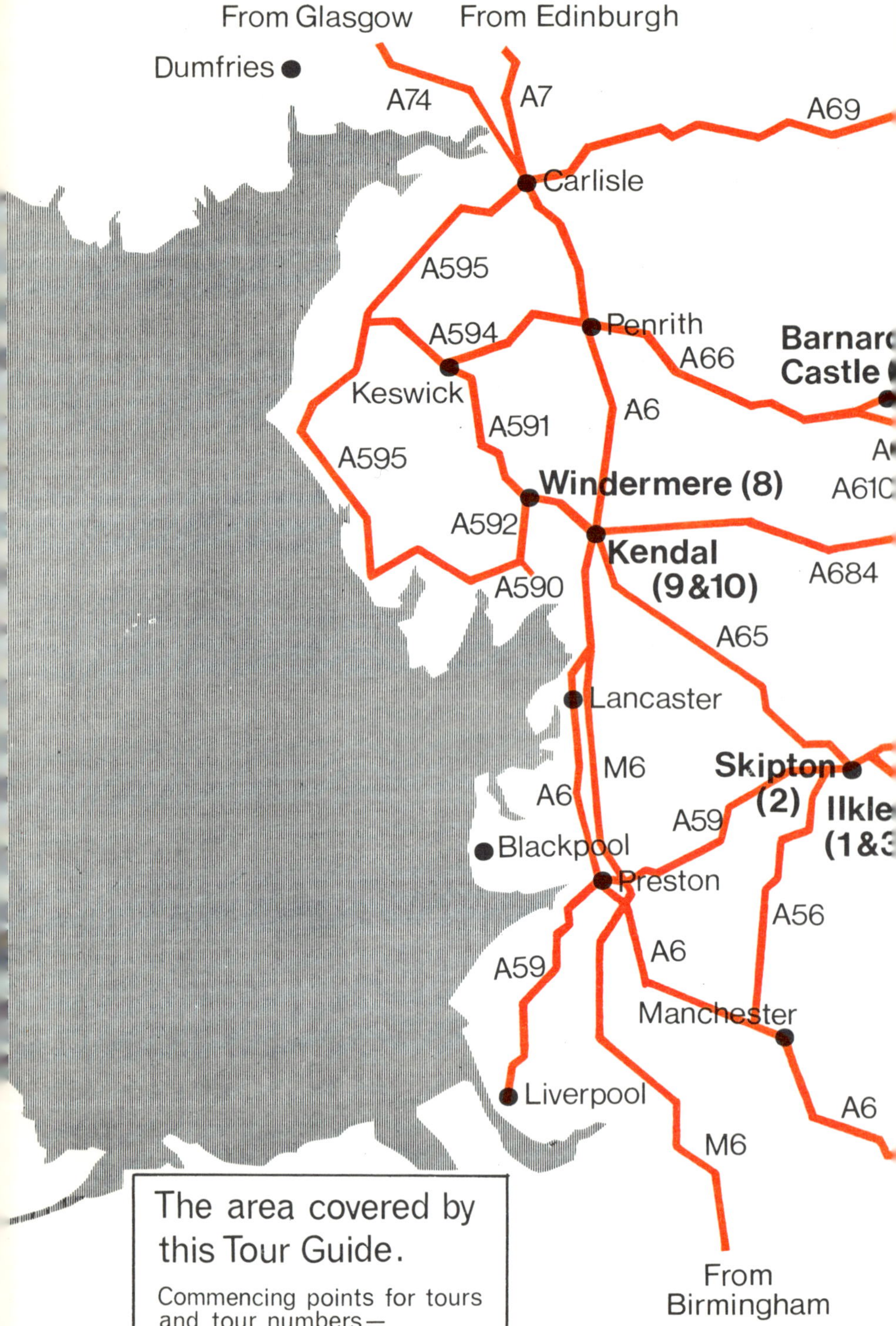

The area covered by this Tour Guide.

Commencing points for tours and tour numbers—
Skipton(2)

rom
dinburgh
A1
Newcastle
(7)
A1
iddlesbrough
67
Darlington
Scotch Corner
Richmond (5)
Scarborough
Ripon
A61
Harrogate (4)
A59
York
A1079
65
Leeds
A63
Hull
radford
A1
A61
M1
M18
Sheffield
A1
M1
From London
N

Tour 1
94 miles

1. The Yorkshire Dales: Wharfedale and Wensleydale

Three of the first four tours in this book cover the well-known Yorkshire Dales, varied and beautiful valleys penetrating into the eastern side of the great range of Pennine moorlands. This tour takes in two of the best-loved dales, the long, deep-cut Wharfedale and the broad, more pastoral Wensleydale, both with their many delightful villages. It includes also the favoured holiday resorts and spas of Ilkley and Harrogate, the interesting monastic remains of Bolton Priory, Jervaulx Abbey and (especially) Fountains Abbey, the impressive medieval ruins of Middleham Castle, and the model villages of Harewood and Ripley (which also has a castle), as well as the splendid mansion of Harewood House.

Ilkley is a residential town and a favoured holiday resort, once a popular spa, pleasantly situated on the south bank of the Wharfe, in the open lower part of the dale. All Saints', in the older part of the town north of the railway, is a 16th century parish church with three Saxon crosses in the churchyard. The Manor House Museum (admission daily, except Mondays, 10.30 to 12.30 and 2 to 5; October-April, 2 to 5 only), in a Tudor house, with local history and prehistory collections (including many Roman finds), is enclosed by the Roman fort of Olicana, part of which has been excavated. To the south of the town rises Ilkley Moor, part of the long Rombalds Moor, covered with heather and bracken, and with a wealth of prehistoric remains. A fine view of the dale is obtained from the distinctive Cow and Calf Rocks, to the south-east.

From Ilkley by Skipton Road and A65, ascending the Wharfe to Addingham (3 miles), then by B6160 to Bolton Bridge (2½ miles) and on to Bolton Abbey (½ mile).

Bolton Abbey is a village beautifully situated on the Wharfe at the entrance to the loveliest part of the dale. Bolton Priory (admission daily, 9 to dusk) was an Augustinian house refounded in 1151. The 13th century nave of the priory church, on the bank of the river, has probably been used by the parish since it was built. The unfinished west front was begun in 1520; the choir and transepts, altered in the 14th century, remain in ruins. Near by is the mid-19th century Bolton Hall, now used by the Duke of Devonshire as a shooting-lodge, incorporating the 14th century priory gatehouse.

B6160 ascends the wooded dale to Barden Tower (3 miles) and thence to Burnsall (3 miles).

Barden Tower is a massive tower-house of the 15th century, partly restored in 1659 by Lady Anne Clifford, who lived at Skipton Castle, but now in ruins again. Attached to a cottage in the courtyard is a 17th century chapel. Burnsall is a charming village on a fine reach of the Wharfe, on the edge of the limestone district of Craven. It has a 16th century church with a late-Saxon or

Norman font and a mellowed 17th century house built as the grammar school.

B6160 goes on up Wharfedale to Linton (2½ miles; on the left), where a road from Skipton comes in, and thence to Threshfield (1 mile). Grassington, on Tour 4, is 1 mile to the right from here.

Linton is a secluded village with old houses charmingly grouped round a green divided by a beck which is crossed by an old pack-horse bridge. The interesting church, showing work of the 12th-16th centuries, is ½-mile away, beside the river.

B6160 on up the dale to Kilnsey (2½ miles) and thence to Kettlewell (3 miles).

Kilnsey is a hamlet and fishing resort under the precipitous limestone buttress of Kilnsey Crag, and south of the entrance to Littondale, the valley of the Skirfare, up which a quiet road runs to the attractive villages of Arncliffe and Litton. Kettlewell is a delightful village with many old whitewashed houses and inns, below Great Whernside (2310 feet). About 1 mile up the Park Gill Beck is the foot of Park Rash, a noted motor test climb.

B6160 on up the narrowing dale to Buckden (3½ miles).

Buckden is the highest village in Wharfedale and has the last inn in the dale serving meals. It stands ¾ mile below the head of the strath, at the junction of the Cray Beck with the Wharfe, at the foot of Langstrothdale. Hubberholme, on Tour 4, is 1 mile left.

B6160 ascends steeply past the hamlet of Cray (1½ miles) to the top of the Kidstones Pass (1½ miles), then descends steadily through Bishopdale to West Burton (6 miles).

The Kidstones Pass (1392 feet) is on the watershed between Wharfedale and Wensleydale. It lies between Buckden Pike (2302 feet), to the south, and Stake Moss (1836 feet), and commands a wide view over the Pennine moorlands. West Burton is an attractive village with a long green, near the foot of Bishopdale at its opening into Wensleydale, across which there is a fine view of Bolton Castle (on Tour 3).

B6160 on for 1½ miles to join A684 (from Hawes), which runs east to West Witton (2½ miles more).

West Witton is a pleasant small village on the southern slopes of Wensleydale, at the foot of the prominent Penhill (1792 feet), which rises between the Walden Valley and Coverdale.

A684 on to Wensley (2 miles) and thence to Leyburn (1 mile).

Wensley, which gives its name to the dale (the valley of the Ure), is an attractive village on a slope above the water, with an interesting 13th-14th century church that has a variety of 16th-17th century woodwork, a unique wooden reliquary (perhaps of the 14th century), and the magnificent 14th century Flemish brass of a priest. Leyburn is an old market town with a wide square, built high up on a shelf above the north side of Wensleydale. A footpath leads west along The Shawl, a green terrace from which there is an enticing view of the dale.

A684 on for ½ mile, then A6108 (right), crossing the Ure, to Middleham (1½ miles more).

Middleham, well known for its racing stables, is an old grey-stone town with hilly and irregular streets, on the slope of a hill above the Ure. The 14th-15th century church contains the fine monumental graveslab of a 16th century abbot of Jervaulx. The impressive Castle (admission 9.30 to 4 in November-February, to 5.30, or to 7, in May-September; Sundays from 2), the stronghold of the Earl of Warwick, the 'king-maker', and a favourite retreat of Richard III, has a massive Norman keep, enclosed in the 13th century by an outer wall which has left only a restricted courtyard.

A6108 on to East Witton (1½ miles) and thence to Jervaulx Abbey (1½ miles).

East Witton is a characteristic village with old grey-stone cottages, built round a tree-shaded green, above the junction of the Cover with the Ure. Jervaulx Abbey (admission weekdays, 9 to 6), pleasantly situated near the river, was a Cistercian monastery founded in the 12th century for monks from Savigny, in France. Little survives of the church, but the remains of the domestic buildings are extensive and include the chapter house, the dormitory and the infirmary.

A6108 on to Masham (5½ miles), then by an unclassified road south, on the west bank of the Ure, to Kirkby Malzeard (4½ miles).

Masham is an old agricultural town with a huge market place and factories producing Wensleydale cheese. The church, mainly of the 15th century, has a partly Norman steeple, and in the churchyard is a Saxon cross-shaft. Kirkby Malzeard, in a valley below the edge of the Pennine moorlands, has a church that is partly of the 13th century, with a fine Norman doorway, and likewise makes Wensleydale cheese.

Unclassified road on to Winksley (2½ miles) and thence (crossing B6265) to Fountains Abbey (2½ miles).

Fountains Abbey (admission daily, 9.30 to 4 in November-February, to 5.30, or to 7, in May-September; Sundays from 2 in winter), in the verdant valley of the Skell, was founded in 1132 for Cistercians, and the ruins, of the 12th-16th centuries, are the most extensive and most complete of any abbey in England, and perhaps the most beautifully situated. Notable features are the splendid late-Norman nave of the church; the 13th century presbytery and Chapel of the Nine Altars, a masterpiece of delicacy; the massive 15th century transeptal tower; the magnificent Cellarium, 300 feet long, on the west of the cloisters; and the impressive Refectory, to the south. Fountains Hall (admission Easter-October, daily, 10 to 6), close by the west gate, is a well-preserved Jacobean mansion with period furniture and tapestries. A footpath, passing the abbey, leads through the valley to the beautiful park of Studley Royal, laid out in the 18th century, an outstanding example of formal landscaping, with classical temples and statuary.

Unclassified road on to Markington (3 miles) and thence left to Wormald Green (1 mile); thence by A61 (right) to Ripley (3 miles).

Ripley is described in Tour 3 (page 19).

A61 on to Harrogate (3½ miles) which is entered by Ripon Road.

Harrogate is a favoured residential town and health resort, on an airy plateau, famous for the great variety of its mineral springs. The Royal Baths, built in 1897 but several times enlarged, contain the bathing and medicinal treatment establishment, to which all the waters are now tapped, and includes also a large winter garden. The Royal Hall (1903) has a theatre and is used for festivals of music and drama. The delightful Valley Gardens close by are noted for their floral displays. The Royal Pump Room (admission 11 to 7, Sundays 2 to 5, but open week-ends only in winter), built in 1842, contains the old sulphur well and an interesting museum of local history. Near the large common known as The Stray, to the south, is the Corporation Art Gallery (admission 10 to 7 or dusk, Sundays 2 to 5), which arranges good loan exhibitions.

A61 leaves Harrogate by Leeds Road, crossing The Stray (see above), and goes on to Pannal (2½ miles), then crosses the Wharfe to Harewood (5 miles).

Harewood is a model village of the 18th century at the gates of Harewood House (admission daily, Easter-September, Sundays in October, 11 to 6), the home of the Earl of Harewood, cousin of the Queen. This splendid mansion was built between 1759 and 1771 by John Carr and Robert Adam, and altered in the 19th century by Sir Charles Barry. It has delicate plaster ceilings, Chippendale and other fine furniture, and a superb collection of Italian and English paintings. In the beautiful park, which was laid out by 'Capability' Brown in the 18th century, is the 15th century Parish Church, with interesting monuments, including that of Chief Justice Gascoigne, who is said by Shakespeare to have committed the Prince of Wales (later Henry V) to prison for contempt of court. Harewood Castle, to the north of the village, is a 14th century tower-house.

A61 back (towards Harrogate) for 1 mile, then A659 (left) to Pool (4½ miles) and thence to Otley (3½ miles).

Otley, on the south bank of the Wharfe, is an old market and manufacturing town with a restored 15th century church containing monuments of the Fairfax and Fawkes families. A plaque in the Market Place marks the site of the birthplace (1718) of Thomas Chippendale, the cabinet-maker.

A660 on to Burley-in-Wharfedale (2½ miles) then A65 (right) to Ilkley (3½ miles) which is entered by Leeds Road.

2. Across the Lower Pennines to Ribblesdale and Lunesdale

This tour starts in the upper pastoral reach of Airedale, takes in Haworth, a village famous for its association with the Brontë sisters, crosses the wild Pennine moorlands to Lancashire and the lower Ribble valley, then goes over the lonely moors of the Forest of Bowland to Lancaster. It continues up the green Lunesdale or Lonsdale, then from Ingleton recrosses the Pennines via Settle to Airedale once more. Its varied interest includes the castles of Skipton and Lancaster, the abbey remains at Whalley, the fine churches at Lancaster and Kirkby Lonsdale, and the caves and waterfalls near Ingleton, as well as the interesting museum at Settle, an old town in the Craven limestone district.

Skipton, the gateway to the limestone district of Craven, is a delightful old market town north of the Aire, with a broad tree-lined main street. The Craven Museum (admission Monday and Wednesday-Friday 2 to 5, Saturdays 10 to 12 and 1.30 to 4.30), in the public library, has collections illustrating local history and natural history. The Parish Church, mainly of the 15th century, has excellent woodwork and tombs of the Cliffords, Earls of Cumberland. Skipton Castle (admission weekdays 10 to dusk, Sundays 2 to dusk; conducted parties on the hour), the home of the Cliffords and their descendants from 1309 until 1955, is partly of the 14th century and has a gatehouse with huge round towers. The long banqueting hall on the north side of the inner court is part of a Tudor extension built for the 1st Earl of Cumberland, and the castle was much altered in the 17th century by Lady Anne Clifford, Countess of Pembroke.

From Skipton by Keighley Road and A629 through the Aire valley to Kildwick (4½ miles).

Kildwick, where the Aire is crossed by a bridge that is partly medieval, has a long 14th-15th century church. Kildwick Hall, to the north, is a 16th century manor house.

A629 on over the river to Steeton (2 miles) and thence to Keighley (3 miles).

Keighley is a market and textile-manufacturing town with wide streets, at the foot of the Worth Valley. Cliffe Castle (admission weekdays 10.30 to 5.30 or dusk, Sundays 2 to 5 or dusk), a house of 1878 in a fine park to the north-west, contains a well-arranged museum and art gallery, with local ' bygones ', craft workshops, and a good collection of musical instruments. East Riddlesden Hall (admission daily, except Monday, 2 to 6 or dusk), to the north-east near the Bradford road, is a characteristic 17th century manor house with period furniture. In the grounds is a medieval tithe-barn.

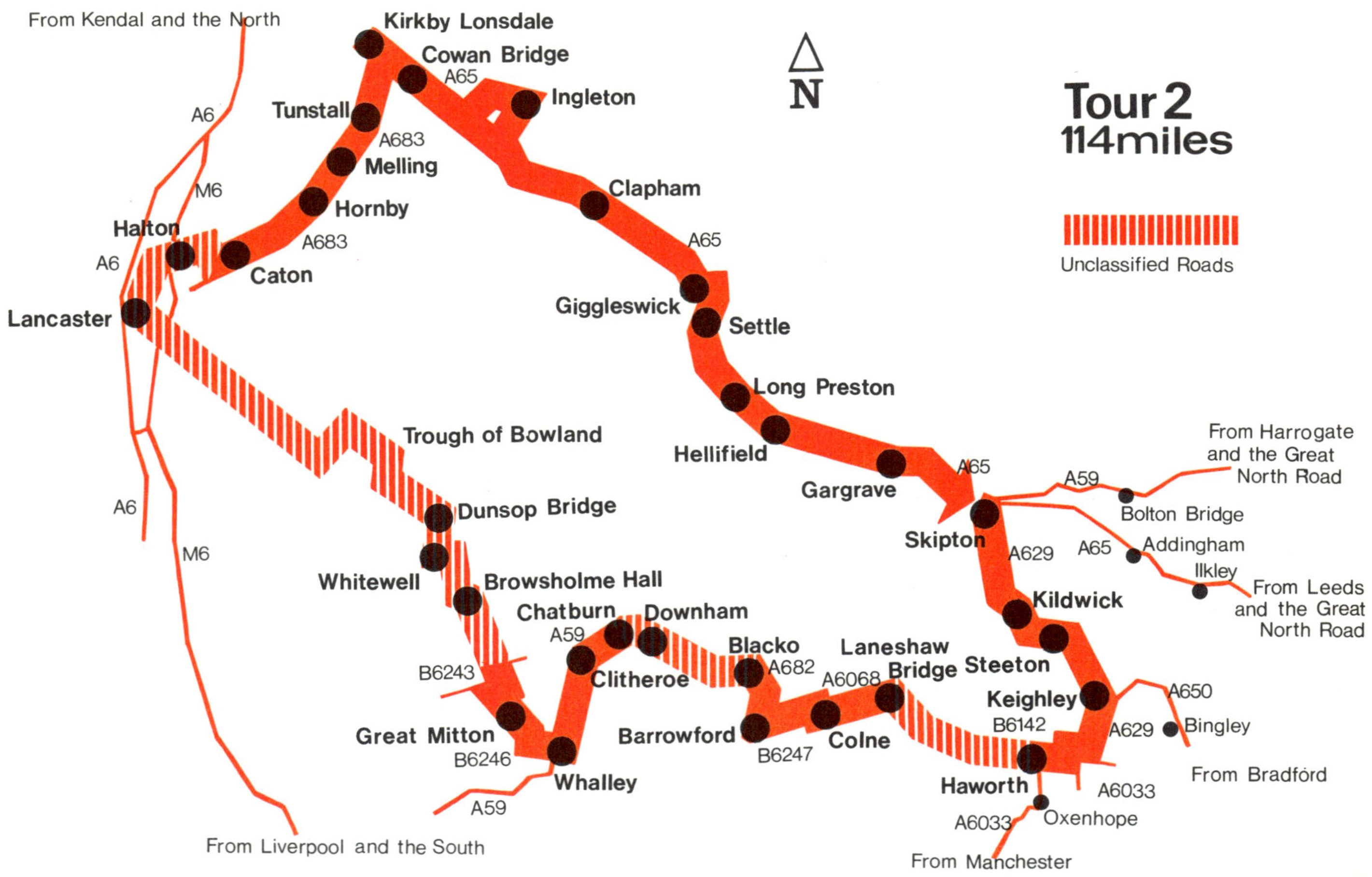

Tour 2
114miles
Unclassified Roads
N
From Kendal and the North
Kirkby Lonsdale
Cowan Bridge
A65
Ingleton
Tunstall
A683
Melling
Hornby
A683
Caton
Halton
A6
M6
A6
Lancaster
Clapham
A65
Giggleswick
Settle
Long Preston
Hellifield
Gargrave
A65
Skipton
Trough of Bowland
Dunsop Bridge
Whitewell
Browsholme Hall
Chatburn
A59
Downham
Clitheroe
Blacko
A682
Laneshaw
Bridge
A6068
Steeton
Kildwick
A629
Keighley
B6142
Haworth
B6243
Great Mitton
B6246
Whalley
A59
Barrowford
B6247
Colne
A6
M6
From Liverpool and the South
From Harrogate
and the Great
North Road
A59
Bolton Bridge
A65
Addingham
Ilkley
From Leeds
and the Great
North Road
A650
A629
Bingley
From Bradford
A6033
Oxenhope
A6033
From Manchester

A629 up the Worth Valley for 2 miles, then A6033 (right) for ½ mile and B6142 (right again) to Haworth (½ mile more).

Haworth is an old-fashioned stone-built village with steep cobbled streets, on the edge of the moors made famous by *Jane Eyre* and *Wuthering Heights*. The church, mostly rebuilt in 1881, contains the graves of Charlotte and Emily Brontë. Above the churchyard is the 18th century Parsonage to which the Rev. Patrick Brontë brought his family in 1820. Now the Brontë Parsonage Museum (admission 11 to 4.45 or 5.45, Sundays from 2; closed on Fridays in winter), it holds many relics, manuscripts and books relating to the sisters.

Unclassified road on from Haworth church and over the wild moorlands of the Forest of Trawden, crossing the Lancashire boundary, to Laneshaw Bridge (8 miles), then A6068 (left) to Colne (2 miles).

Colne, on a ridge above the valley of the Colne Water, is an old-established market and textile-manufacturing town. The restored 16th century church has good timber roofs, and in the churchyard are the unusual mobile stocks.

A56 on for ½ mile, then B6247 (right, i.e. west) for Barrowford (1½ miles).

Barrowford, on the Pendle Water, with cotton mills, lies east of the moorland Forest of Pendle, which rises to the great dome of Pendle Hill (1831 feet).

A682 (right) through Blacko (2 miles), then by an unclassified road (left) across the steep northern slopes of Pendle Hill (see above) to Downham (4½ miles).

Downham is a delightful stone-built village, embosomed among trees in a secluded valley, with a 16th century manor house.

Unclassified road on to Chatburn (1½ miles), then A59 (left) to Clitheroe (2 miles).

Clitheroe is a market town and an old-established borough, on a hill above the Ribble valley, and is the farthest north of the Lancashire cotton towns. Commandingly placed on a limestone rock is the small keep of a Norman Castle.

A59 on, east of the Ribble, to Whalley (4 miles).

Whalley is a village on the Calder where it emerges into the pleasant valley of the Ribble. The interesting church, mainly of the 13th century, has 15th century additions and a wealth of old woodwork, including an elaborate family pew, and 15th century stalls from the abbey, and in the churchyard are three Saxon crosses. Whalley Abbey (admission to grounds, daily, 10 to dusk) was a Cistercian foundation of the 13th century. The chief remains are two 14th-15th century gatehouses and part of the cloister; the restored 16th century abbot's lodging is now a conference house of the Diocese of Blackburn.

B6246 across the Ribble and through Great Mitton (3 miles) then B6243 (right) and by an unclassified road (left) to Browsholme Hall (4½ miles).

Great Mitton has an interesting church, mainly of about 1300, with a 15th century tower, 15th-16th century woodwork, and family monuments of the Shireburns, who lived at Stonyhurst, an Elizabethan mansion to the west, beyond the Hodder, now the nucleus of a well-known Roman Catholic college. Browsholme Hall (admission Easter to mid-October, Thursday, Saturday and Sunday, 2 to 6.30), the home of the Parkers, verderers of the Forest of Bowland (see below) at least since the 14th century, is a Tudor house altered in the 17th and 18th centuries, and containing relics from the forest.

Unclassified road on to Whitewell (2½ miles) and up the valley of the Hodder to Dunsop Bridge (2 miles), then (left) ascending to the Trough of Bowland (3 miles).

The Forest of Bowland. Beyond Dunsop Bridge the road traverses this tract of wild and lonely moorland, lying to the west of the main Pennine chain, and penetrated by attractive valleys. The road climbs from one of these to the Trough of Bowland, a narrow pass that reaches about 1000 feet, between the Hodder and Wyre valleys. On the west side there are fine views across Morecambe Bay to the Lakeland mountains.

Unclassified road on across the head-waters of the Wyre, then over the side of Abbeystead Fell, descending thence to Lancaster (12 miles) which is entered by Wyresdale Road and East Road.

Lancaster is a former county town on the tidal Lune, an old-established borough and a market centre, with many fine 18th century buildings. The Castle (admission weekdays at 10.30, 11, 11.30, 2, 2.30, 3 and 3.30), on a hill above the river, is of the 11th century and later. It was strengthened by John of Gaunt, Duke of Lancaster, and much altered after 1788, and houses the law courts and a prison. The excellent Priory Church close by is mainly of the 15th century and has richly-carved 14th century stalls. The Old Town Hall, in Market Street, now contains the interesting Lancaster Museum (admission weekdays, 10 to 5.30), with collections of antiquities and historical relics.

A6 north, crossing the Lune by Skerton Bridge, then by an unclassified road (right) to Halton (2 miles); then across the river near the Crook o' Lune and by A683 (left) through Caton (2½ miles) and on to Hornby (4½ miles).

Halton. In the churchyard here is an 11th century cross carved with scenes from the Norse saga of Sigurd the Volsung. The Crook o' Lune is a sharp bend of the river that was painted by Turner, in the most beautiful stretch of the valley. Hornby, charmingly situated on a tributary, the Wenning, has a church with an unusual octagonal tower and the dominating keep of a Castle, both built in the 16th century by Sir Edward Stanley.

A683 on through the green Lunesdale to Melling (2 miles) and thence to Tunstall (2 miles).

Melling has good 18th century houses, including the Hall (now a hotel), and a 15th century church containing a set of musical instruments once used to accompany the choir. Tunstall is the 'Brocklebridge' of *Jane Eyre* and the 15th century church is that attended by the pupils at Cowan Bridge (see below).

A683 on for 3 miles, then A65 (left) across the Lune for Kirkby Lonsdale (½ mile more).

Kirkby Lonsdale is an old agricultural town with large cattle and sheep markets. The interesting church is partly of the 14th-15th centuries, but has Norman nave arcades and west doorway and good 13th century work in the chancel. The river is crossed above the modern road bridge by the picturesque Devil's Bridge, probably of the late-15th century.

A65 back (i.e. east) across the Lune and on to Cowan Bridge (2 miles); then on again for 3½ miles, and B6255 (left) for Ingleton (½ mile more).

Cowan Bridge is a hamlet on the Leck Beck, beside which is the old building of the Clergy Daughters' School. Charlotte Brontë, who was a pupil here, has described the school in unsavoury terms in *Jane Eyre*. Ingleton stands at the junction of two becks, the Greta and the Kingsdale Beck, which above the village flow through impressive limestone ravines, often called the Ingleton Glens, noted for their waterfalls. Among the finest and most accessible of the many caverns and pot-holes in the district are Skirwith Cave and the White Scar Caves (admission daily to both, in summer), to the north-east near the Hawes road. Farther north-east rises Ingleborough (2373 feet), one of the highest and most distinctive of the Pennine hills.

Unclassified road south for ½ mile to rejoin A65, then below the southern slopes of Ingleborough to Clapham (4 miles more) and thence under Giggleswick Scar to Giggleswick (5½ miles).

Clapham is a sequestered village in a wooded valley enclosed by a limestone district interesting for its caves and pot-holes. Ingleborough Cave, over 1 mile north by footpath, has an extensive series of passages and chambers. Giggleswick, on the west bank of the Ribble, is an old-fashioned village with 17th-18th century houses and a fine church of about 1500. Giggleswick School, to the west, with a prominent domed chapel, is a public school founded in 1512. To the north-west, beside the Clapham road under the long crag of Giggleswick Scar, is the celebrated Ebbing and Flowing Well.

A65 on across the Ribble to Settle (1 mile).

Settle is a delightful old town and market centre in Ribblesdale, at the point where the river breaks through the limestone outcrops of Craven. It has narrow streets with characteristic 17th and 18th century houses. At Townhead, to the north of the church, is a fascinating Museum (admission, usually on application) of the geology and history of the Craven Caves. Roads with steep hills cross the fells on the east to Malham Tarn and Kirkby Malham (on Tour 3).

A65 on down Ribblesdale to Long Preston (4 miles) and thence to Hellifield (2 miles).

Hellifield is a village on the watershed of the Pennines (the ' Backbone of England ') between the Ribble, which flows west to the Irish Sea, and the Aire, which flows east towards the North Sea.

A65 on into Airedale for Gargrave (5 miles), and thence to Skipton (4 miles), which is entered by Gargrave Road and Water Street.

3. The Yorkshire Dales: Wensleydale and Ribblesdale

This tour takes in practically the whole of Wensleydale as well as a large part of upper Ribblesdale. Starting from lower Wharfedale, it includes, besides many charming villages, the famous holiday and residential town of Ilkley, the small but interesting cathedral city of Ripon, the beautifully-situated remains of Jervaulx Abbey, the dominating Bolton Castle, and the wide falls on the Ure near Aysgarth, as well as the small market town of Hawes, from which it crosses the watershed of the Pennine moorlands, returning via Malham, in the Craven district, with its remarkable limestone features, and Skipton, an old market town with another interesting castle.

Ilkley is described at the beginning of Tour 1 (page 9).

From Ilkley by Brook Street and the bridge over the Wharfe, then by an unclassified road (right), north of the river, to Askwith (4 miles), and thence to Otley Bridge (2½ miles). B6451 (left) to Farnley Hall (1½ miles), then by an unclassified road (right) to Leathley (1½ miles).

Farnley Hall, the home of the Fawkes family (of whom the notorious Guy Fawkes was a member), is an Elizabethan house with a splendid extension by John Carr of York (1790). It contains paintings by J. M. W. Turner, who was a frequent visitor here. Leathley, a pleasant hamlet on the Washburn near its junction with the Wharfe, has a church with an early-Norman tower which retains its original ironbound door.

B6161 (left) to Beckwithshaw (5 miles), for Harlow Car.

Harlow Car. Here are the large ornamental Gardens (admission daily, 9 to dusk) and the fine woodlands of the Northern Horticultural Society.

B6161 on from Beckwithshaw to Killinghall (3½ miles), then A61 (left) to Ripley (1½ miles).

Ripley is a model village, mostly of the early-19th century, and has a 14th-15th century church containing monuments of the Ingilby family, who still live at the Castle (admission May-September, Sundays and Bank Holidays, 2 to 6; gardens also on Saturdays from June, 2 to 6), which is of the 15th century and later, and has graceful interiors. Oliver Cromwell spent the night here after his victory at the Battle of Marston Moor (1644).

A61 on to Wormald Green (3 miles) and thence to Ripon (4 miles).

Ripon is an old market town with congested streets and interesting houses, on the Skell, a tributary of the Ure. In the spacious Market Place the 'wakeman', or watchman, by ancient custom, still blows a horn at 9 o'clock each evening. The Wakeman's

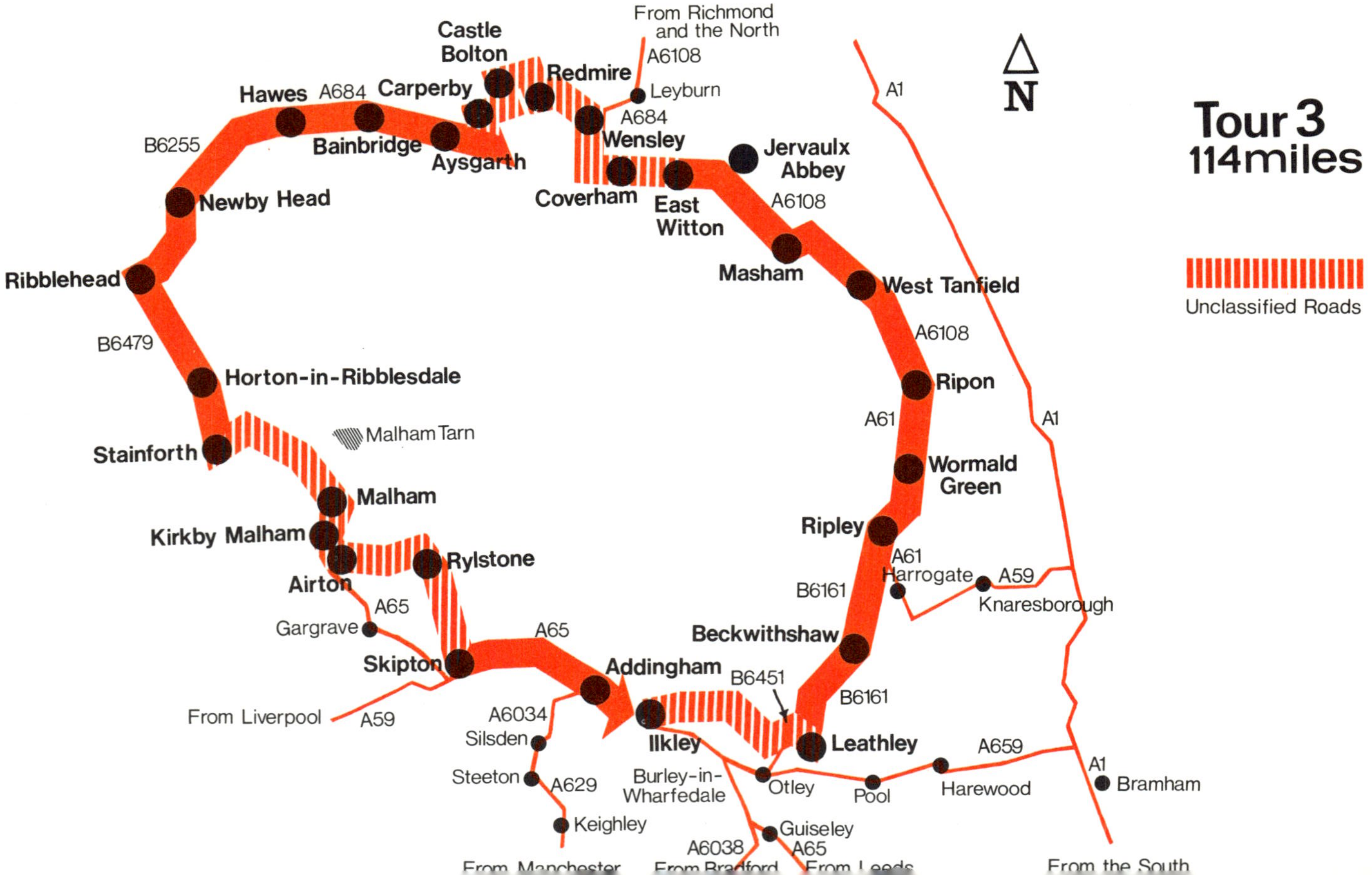
Tour 3
114miles
N
Unclassified Roads
From Richmond and the North
A6108
Leyburn
A684
Castle Bolton
Redmire
Wensley
Carperby
Hawes
A684
Bainbridge
Aysgarth
B6255
Newby Head
Coverham
East Witton
Jervaulx Abbey
A6108
Masham
West Tanfield
A6108
Ripon
A61
Wormald Green
Ripley
A61
Harrogate
A59
Knaresborough
B6161
Beckwithshaw
B6161
B6451
Leathley
A659
Harewood
Pool
Otley
A1
Bramham
A1
A1
Ribblehead
B6479
Horton-in-Ribblesdale
Malham Tarn
Stainforth
Malham
Kirkby Malham
Airton
Rylstone
A65
Gargrave
Skipton
A65
Addingham
Ilkley
From Liverpool
A59
A6034
Silsden
Steeton
A629
Keighley
Burley-in-Wharfedale
Guiseley
A6038
A65
From Manchester
From Bradford
From Leeds
From the South

House, a medieval timber-framed building on the south side, now contains a folk Museum (admission weekdays, except Wednesday afternoons, 9 to 5). The Cathedral or Minster, in Kirkgate, is one of the smaller medieval cathedrals, but shows a variety of architectural styles, from the 12th century onward, and retains the original Saxon crypt of the monastic church built by St. Wilfrid in the 7th century. Notable features are the splendid 15th century stone rood-screen and the graceful late-15th century choir stalls with canopies and misericords. Above the chapter house, in an unusual position, is the Lady Chapel, now housing the cathedral library.

A61 on for ½ mile, then A6108 to West Tanfield (5½ miles) and thence to Masham (4 miles; also on Tour 1).

West Tanfield is an attractive village on the north bank of the Ure. The restored 15th century church has fine modern woodcarving by Robert Thompson, a Yorkshire craftsman, and effigies of the Marmions, who lived at the near-by castle, of which the picturesque 15th century gatehouse survives. Masham is an old agricultural town with a huge market place and factories producing Wensleydale cheese. The church, mainly of the 15th century, has a partly Norman steeple, and in the churchyard is a Saxon cross-shaft.

A6108 on through the open lower valley of the Ure to Jervaulx Abbey (5½ miles) and thence to East Witton (1½ miles).

Jervaulx Abbey (admission weekdays, 9 to 6), pleasantly situated near the river, was a Cistercian monastery founded in the 12th century for monks from Savigny, in France. Little survives of the church, but the remains of the domestic buildings are extensive and include the chapter house, the dormitory and the infirmary. East Witton is a characteristic village with old grey-stone cottages, built round a tree-shaded green, above the junction of the Cover with the Ure.

Unclassified road on, along the south side of Coverdale, then across the river to Coverham (2½ miles), and thence over Middleham Low Moor (noted for its racehorse gallops) to Wensley (3 miles).

Coverham is a hamlet in a delightful position at the foot of the upper part of Coverdale, with remains of a 13th century abbey built into an 18th century house. Wensley, which gives its name to the dale of the Ure, is an attractive village on a slope above the river, with an interesting 13th-14th century church which has a variety of 16th-17th century woodwork, a unique wooden reliquary (perhaps of the 14th century), and the magnificent 14th century Flemish brass of a priest. Leyburn, on Tour 1, is 1 mile to the right, on A684.

Unclassified road west, on the north side of Wensleydale, to Redmire (3½ miles) and thence (right) to Castle Bolton (1 mile).

Redmire is an attractive village in an open part of the dale, with a good view of the prominent Penhill opposite. Castle Bolton, on a shelf above the dale, is an old-world village with a wide green, dominated by Bolton Castle, a towering 14th century stronghold, where Mary, Queen of Scots, was imprisoned for six months after her flight from Scotland in 1568. The restored south-west wing, which commands a fine view up the dale, contains a small museum of 'bygones' and a reproduction of a 19th century Wensleydale kitchen.

Unclassified road on west, through the dale, to Carperby (2½ miles) and thence south, crossing the Ure at Aysgarth Falls (1 mile).

Carperby is another characteristic stone-built village. At Aysgarth Falls the river drops over an impressive series of limestone ledges, above a 16th century bridge. The rebuilt church of Aysgarth, above on the south bank, has a splendid 15th century rood-screen.

A684 (right) through the plain village of Aysgarth (½ mile) and on to Bainbridge (4 miles).

Bainbridge is a pleasant village built round a spacious green, with the mounds of a Roman fort on the east of the river Bain. The old custom is maintained of sounding a horn every winter's night, at 9 p.m., to guide benighted travellers on the fells. To the south-east rises the distinctive flat-topped hill of Addlebrough (1564 feet).

A684 west up the dale to Hawes (4½ miles).

Hawes is an old grey market town noted for its sheep sales and Wensleydale cheese. Hardrow Force (on Tour 4) is about 1 mile north, beyond the river.

B6255 on from the west end of Hawes, ascending the remote Widdale, among the Pennine fells, to Newby Head (6½ miles) and thence down into the upper Ribble valley for Ribblehead (3½ miles).

Newby Head (1434 feet) is a farm on the watershed between the Widdale Beck, which flows north to Wensleydale, and the Gayle Beck, which descends south to Ribblesdale, and near the junction of a road to Dentdale (Tour 6). Ribblehead, lower down and west of the Gayle Beck, has a solitary station on the exhilarating railway that crosses the moors from Settle to Kirkby Stephen.

B6479 (left) to Horton-in-Ribblesdale (5½ miles) and thence to Stainforth (3½ miles) from which Settle (on Tour 2) is 2½ miles farther on.

Horton-in-Ribblesdale is a quarrying village with a rustic 12th and 15th century church which has a Norman font. To the north-east rises Penyghent (2273 feet), one of the most striking in form of the Pennine hills. Stainforth is an attractive village with a 17th century pack-horse bridge over the Ribble.

Unclassified road (with steep hills) north-east to Sannet Hall (1 mile), on the limestone uplands, and thence (right) for Malham Tarn (3½ miles).

Malham Tarn is a quiet upland lake, about 1200 feet up, in a shallow depression on a wide green tableland. Charles Kingsley wrote part of *The Water Babies* (which is set in this district) at Tarn House, on the north side, now a field-study centre.

Unclassified road (right) with a steep descent past Malham Cove (see below) to Malham (2½ miles).

Malham is an attractive village (popular at week-ends) on the Aire, which issues, a full-grown stream, from a subterranean course, at the foot of Malham Cove, an amphitheatre of sheer rock walls about 300 feet high. The road east from Malham leads towards Gordale Scar, a deep narrow ravine with impressive waterfalls, hemmed in by bold crags. Like the Cove, it is the result of the displacement of the mountain limestone known as the Craven Fault.

Unclassified road south from Malham to Kirkby Malham (1½ miles).

Kirkby Malham, in a fold of the hills west of the Aire, has a Tudor church with 17th-18th century pews.

Unclassified road on to Airton (1½ miles), then left across the river and through Hetton to Rylstone (4½ miles).

Rylstone is an attractive village in the limestone gap between the Wharfe and the Aire.

B6265 (right) to Skipton (4½ miles).

Skipton is a delightful old market town north of the Aire, with a broad tree-lined main street. The Craven Museum (admission Monday and Wednesday-Friday 2 to 5, Saturdays 10 to 12 and 1.30 to 4.30), in the public library, has collections illustrating local history and natural history. The Parish Church, mainly of the 15th century, has excellent woodwork and tombs of the Cliffords, Earls of Cumberland. Skipton Castle (admission week-days 10 to dusk, Sundays 2 to dusk: conducted parties on the hour), the home of the Cliffords and their descendants from 1309 until 1955, is partly of the 14th century and has a gatehouse with huge round towers. The long banqueting hall on the north side of the inner court is part of a Tudor extension built for the 1st Earl of Cumberland, and the castle was much altered in the 17th century by Lady Anne Clifford, Countess of Pembroke.

A65, leaving Skipton by Newmarket Street and Otley Road, to Addingham (6 miles), in the lower part of Wharfedale, and thence to Ilkley (3 miles), which is entered by Skipton Road.

Tour 4
116 miles

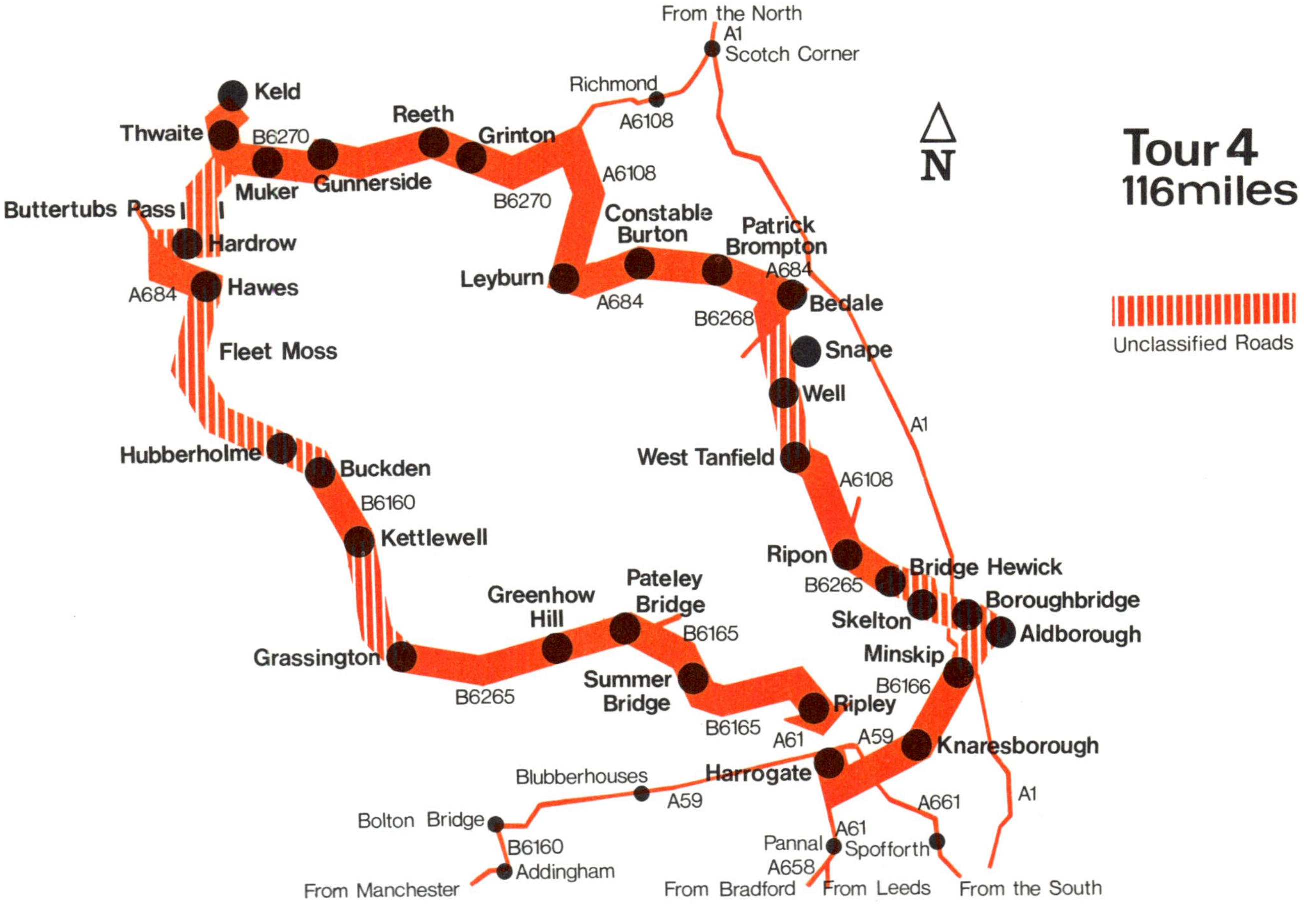

4. The Yorkshire Dales: Swaledale and Wharfedale

This tour, notable for its many interesting churches and delightful villages, runs at first through the rich pastoral country of the Vale of York and takes in the old town of Knaresborough, the Roman remains at Aldborough, the fine Georgian mansion of Newby Hall, and the engaging little cathedral city of Ripon. It ascends Swaledale, the northernmost and one of the most beautiful of the Yorkshire Dales, and includes also the old market towns of Bedale, Leyburn and Hawes, from the last of which the tour crosses the high moorlands of the Pennines to the upper reach of Wharfedale. From Grassington, the ' capital ' of the dale, it crosses the moors again to the charming lower part of Nidderdale.

Harrogate is described in Tour 1 (page 12).

From Harrogate by Leeds Road (A61) to The Stray, then by York Place (left) and A59 to Knaresborough (3½ miles).

Knaresborough is an old market town, with many 18th century houses, finely situated on a cliff high above the river Nidd, which flows through a deep ravine. In a public park are the remains of John of Gaunt's Castle, where Richard II was imprisoned in 1399. The most notable part is the 14th century keep, which served also as a gatehouse. The large 13th-15th century church has good 17th century monuments of the Slingsby family. Near the river, upstream, is the 18th century Conyngham Hall, which has charming grounds with a zoo. From the High Bridge a path follows the river down to the Dropping Well, noted for its petrifying properties, and Mother Shipton's Cave, near by.

B6166 on to Minskip (5½ miles), then by an unclassified road (right) to Aldborough (1½ miles).

Aldborough is a village on the site of the Roman town of Isurium, the cantonal capital of the Brigantes. The visible remains are to the south-west of the 14th-15th century church and behind the Museum (admission 9.30 to 4 in November-February, to 5.30, or to 7, in May-September; Sundays from 2) and the Aldburgh Arms Inn, where there are two tessellated pavements.

Unclassified road west to Boroughbridge (1 mile).

Boroughbridge is a small town, once a busy coaching stage, with several old inns, on the south bank of the Ure, now by-passed by the Great North Road. The Devil's Arrows, to the west and seen from the new road, are three huge gritstone monoliths, probably of the Bronze Age.

A1167 across the river, then by an unclassified road (left) to Skelton (2½ miles).

Skelton, which has an elaborate church of 1876 by William Burges, stands near the gates of Newby Hall (admission Easter-October,

Wednesdays, Thursdays, Saturdays and Sundays, 2 to 7; gardens open daily), a Queen Anne house remodelled in 1765-83 by Robert Adam, with fine portraits and tapestries, in charming gardens reaching down to the north bank of the Ure.

Unclassified road on to Bridge Hewick (2½ miles), then B6265 (left) to Ripon (1½ miles).

Ripon is an old market town with congested streets and interesting houses, on the Skell, a tributary of the Ure. In the spacious Market Place the 'wakeman' or watchman, by ancient custom, still blows a horn at 9 o'clock each evening. The Wakeman's House, a medieval timber-framed building on the south side, now contains a folk Museum (admission weekdays, except Wednesday afternoons, 9 to 5). The Cathedral or Minster, in Kirkgate, is one of the smaller medieval cathedrals, but shows a variety of architectural styles, from the 12th century onward, and retains the original Saxon crypt of the monastic church built by St. Wilfrid in the 7th century. Notable features are the splendid 15th century stone rood-screen and the graceful late-15th century choir stalls, with canopies and misericords. Above the chapter house, in an unusual position, is the Lady Chapel, now housing the cathedral library.

A61 (right) for ½ mile, then A6108 to West Tanfield (5½ miles); then by an unclassified road north to Well (2 miles).

West Tanfield is an attractive village on the north bank of the Ure. The restored 15th century church has fine modern woodcarving by Robert Thompson, the Yorkshire craftsman, and effigies of the Marmions, who lived at the near-by castle, of which the picturesque 15th century gatehouse survives. Well has a restored church, mostly of the 13th-15th centuries, containing part of a mosaic pavement removed from the bath-house of a Roman villa to the west of the village.

Unclassified road on to Snape (2 miles; on the right), then on again to Mile House (1½ miles); then B6268 (right) to Bedale (1½ miles).

Snape has a long green with a beck running through it, and the 15th-16th century quadrangular Castle, partly ruined, of the powerful Neville and Cecil families. Bedale is an old brick-built market town with a wide curving street. At the north end are the 18th century Hall, now containing a Museum of old crafts (admission March-September, Tuesdays, 2 to 4.30; or by appointment), and the 13th-15th century church, which has 14th century wall paintings and medieval effigies of the Fitzalans.

A684 to Patrick Brompton (3½ miles) and thence to Constable Burton (4 miles).

Patrick Brompton has an interesting church with a late-12th century south doorway and north nave arcade and a 14th century south arcade and fine chancel. Constable Burton has a classical Hall designed in 1762 by John Carr of York.

A684 on to reach Wensleydale at Leyburn (3½ miles).

Leyburn is an old market town with a wide square, built high up on a shelf above the north side of Wensleydale. A footpath leads west along The Shawl, a green terrace from which there is an enticing view of the dale.

A6108 north over the watershed between Wensleydale and Swaledale to Halfpenny House (3 miles) and down the valley of the Gill Beck past Downholme into Swaledale (3 miles); then B6270 (left) up the dale (A6108 goes on to Richmond, on Tour 5) to Grinton ($4\frac{1}{2}$ miles) and thence across the Swale to Reeth (1 mile).

Swaledale, the upper course of the Swale, west of Richmond, is the narrowest, deepest and most remote of the Yorkshire Dales, and in many ways the most fascinating. The road through this well-wooded section of it passes opposite Marrick Priory, 12th century remains of which are incorporated in the parish church. Grinton is the centre of a very large parish, with the mother-church of Swaledale, partly Norman, but chiefly of the 15th century. Reeth, built round a large and picturesque green, is an attractive small town (a former lead-mining centre), at the foot of Arkengarthdale, with a thriving sheep market.

B6270 on through Swaledale to Gunnerside (6 miles) and thence to Muker (3 miles).

Gunnerside is one of several small villages and angling resorts in a more open section of the dale. Muker, the former lead-mining capital of upper Swaledale, is a village of enchanting irregularity, with cottages of the dark Pennine gritstone. To the north the dale swings round the base of the steep-sided hill of Kisdon (1636 feet).

B6270 up the tributary Muker Beck nearly to Thwaite (1 mile), then by an unclassified road (left), ascending to the Buttertubs Pass ($2\frac{1}{2}$ miles).

Thwaite is a pleasant hamlet at the south foot of Kisdon from which B6270 goes to regain the Swale, with several pretty waterfalls, near the hamlet of Keld (2 miles farther). The Buttertubs Pass (1726 feet), on the watershed between upper Swaledale and Wensleydale, takes its name from the Buttertubs, a series of deep fissures in the limestone, $\frac{1}{2}$ mile on the north side of the pass, from which a wide view opens of Great Shunner Fell (2340 feet), to the west, and others of the lonely Pennine hills.

Unclassified road on into Wensleydale, then right beyond the farmstead of High Shaw to reach Hardrow ($3\frac{1}{2}$ miles) about $\frac{1}{2}$ mile beyond which A684 leads left to Hawes ($1\frac{1}{2}$ miles more).

Hardrow is a hamlet near the foot of the ravine containing Hardrow Force, a waterfall about 90 feet high (the highest single drop in Yorkshire), but impressive only after wet weather. Hawes is an old grey market town noted for its sheep sales and Wensleydale cheese.

Unclassified road south to Gayle ($\frac{1}{2}$ mile) and up the east side of Sleddale, climbing thence (with one steep section) to Fleet Moss (4 miles), then descending at length into Langstrothdale, the upper reach of Wharfedale, for Hubberholme (6½ miles).

Fleet Moss (1934 feet) is a desolate tract of boggy moorland on the watershed between the upper parts of Wensleydale and Wharfedale. Hubberholme, a remote hamlet near the foot of Langstrothdale, has a rustic church, partly Norman, containing one of the only two rood-lofts in Yorkshire (of the 16th century), as well as pews and stalls by Robert Thompson, the Yorkshire woodcarver.

Unclassified road on, crossing the Wharfe, to Buckden (1 mile), then B6160 down the dale to Kettlewell (3½ miles).

Buckden, the highest village in Wharfedale proper, lies on the level strath, at the foot of the steep slopes of Buckden Pike (2302 feet), which rises to the north-east. Kettlewell is a delightful village with many old whitewashed houses and inns, below Great Whernside (2310 feet). About 1 mile up the Park Gill Beck is the foot of Park Rash, a noted motor test climb.

Unclassified road on the east bank of the Wharfe, below series of limestone scars, to Conistone (3 miles) and thence to Grassington (3 miles).

Grassington, the capital of upper Wharfedale, is a charming small town on the east side of a more open reach of the dale, with a picturesque cobbled street joining two squares.

B6265 on down the north side of the Wharfe to Hebden (1½ miles), then over the breezy Hebden and Appletreewick moors to the Stump Cross Caverns (4 miles) and thence to Greenhow Hill (1½ miles) and on (steep descent) to Pateley Bridge (3½ miles).

Stump Cross Caverns (admission daily in summer; week-ends only in winter) are a series of caves and passages on the edge of the gritstone and the Craven limestone, with interesting stalactite formations. Greenhow Hill, in a district with numerous disused lead workings, now mines fluorspar. Pateley Bridge is an old-fashioned market town with steep streets at the entrance to the narrow and beautiful upper part of Nidderdale.

B6265 down the north side of the valley of the Nidd for 1 mile, then B6165 on to Summer Bridge (2½ miles).

Summer Bridge is a village well situated in the wooded valley. On the moor to the north (reached by a very steep hill) are Brimham Rocks, a remarkable series of gritstone outcrops, some of them over 30 feet high, weathered to fantastic shapes.

B6165 on, north of the Nidd, to Ripley (7 miles), then A61 (right) to Harrogate (3½ miles), which is entered by Ripon Road.

Ripley is described in Tour 3 (page 19).

5. The Pennines, with Teesdale and Swaledale

This tour, through North Yorkshire and crossing the boundaries into Westmorland and County Durham, ascends the lower part of Teesdale, where the imposing waterfall of High Force may be visited, then crosses the wild Pennine moorlands to the broad Vale of Eden. It takes in many charming villages, as well as the fascinating market towns of Richmond, Barnard Castle and Appleby, all of which have splendid castles. At Brough is another interesting castle, and at Barnard Castle the surprising Bowes Museum, full of treasures, in a vast French-style château. From Sedbergh, another old market town, in one of the narrow western dales of the Pennines, the tour recrosses the moors to Hawes, in upper Wensleydale, and then goes over to Swaledale, through which it descends all the way.

Richmond is an enchanting old market town and royal borough, grandly situated on a steep slope above the Swale, near the foot of the dale, with many fine 18th century houses. In the large cobbled Market Place is Holy Trinity Church, now separated from its clock tower by secular buildings, and Friars' Wynd leads north to the delectable Theatre Royal (admission Easter and May-September, daily, 2.30 to 5.30), built in 1788 and the second oldest theatre in Britain. The Norman Castle (admission daily 9.30 to 4, to 5.30, or to 7, May-September; Sundays from 2 only in winter), strikingly placed on a precipice over the river, was begun by the 1st Earl of Richmond, who built the gatehouse, above which the magnificent keep was raised in the 12th century. The restored Parish Church, on the slope to the north, is partly Norman and has 16th century choir stalls from the ruined Easby Abbey, farther downstream.

From Richmond east by A6108, then by an unclassified road (Gallowgate) north for Kirby Hill (4 miles), then an unclassified road on and right to Ravensworth (1½ miles).

Kirby Hill is a charming village on the top of a hill, with a prominent late-14th century church tower. Ravensworth is another attractive village, built in characteristic fashion round a large green, near the 14th century gatehouse and other remains of a once-extensive Castle described in Scott's poem 'Rokeby.'

Unclassified road on for 1 mile, then A66 (left) to Greta Bridge (4 miles).

Greta Bridge is a fine 18th century bridge by John Carr of York, near the entrance to Rokeby Hall, built in 1725-30 for himself by Thomas Robinson, a dilettante architect, and twice visited by Sir Walter Scott, who has praised the beauty of the district in his poem. A lane north of the park leads to the Meeting of the Greta and Tees, painted by Cotman and Turner.

Unclassified road (right), west of the park, past Egglestone Abbey (2 miles).

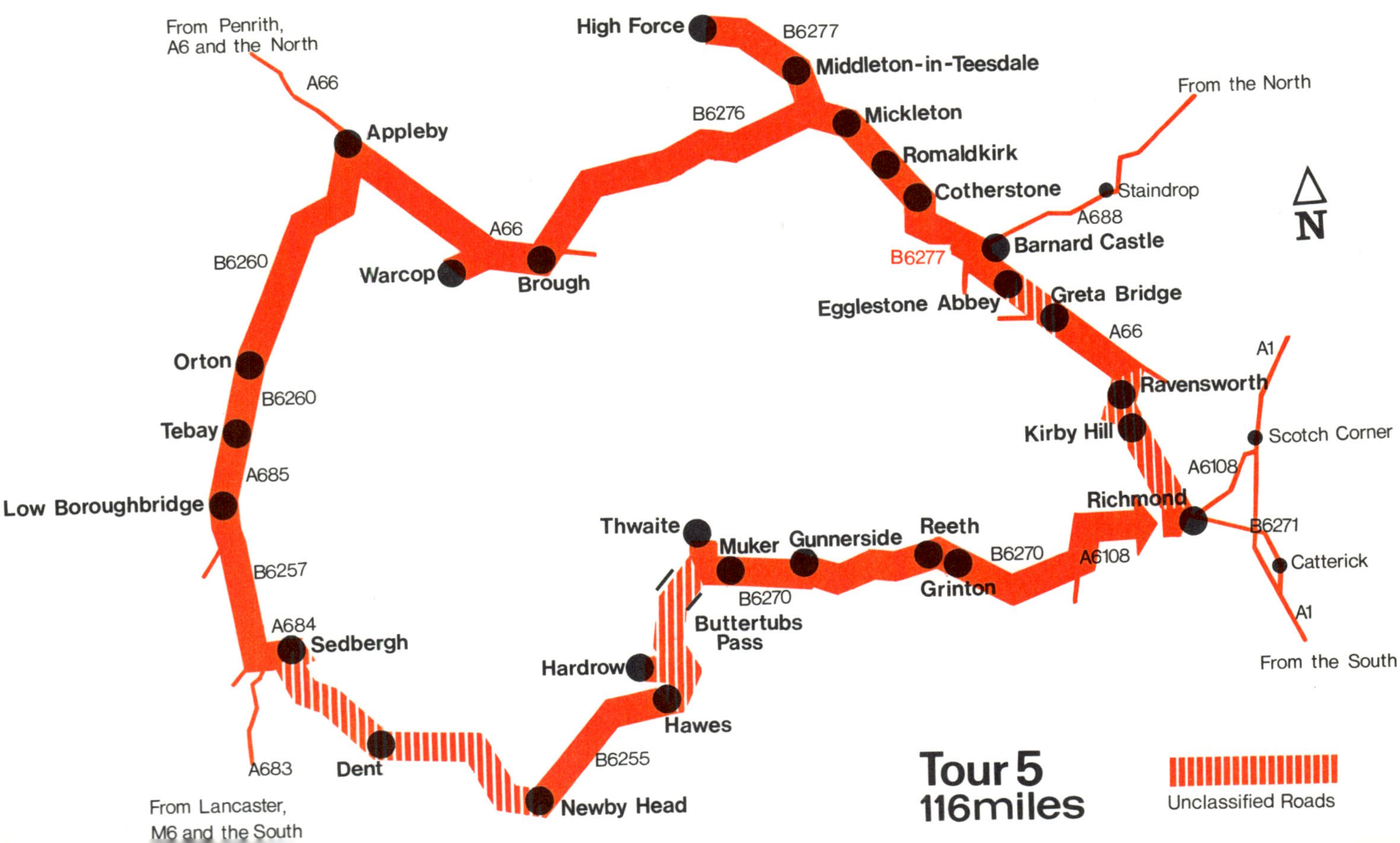

Tour 5
116 miles

Egglestone Abbey (admission as for the castle at Barnard Castle, see below), on a knoll above the Tees, was founded for Premonstratensian canons and the ruins are mostly of the late-12th and 13th centuries. The 18th century Abbey Bridge, to the east, crosses a charming stretch of the rocky river.

B6277 (right) and A67 (right again), crossing the Tees, to Barnard Castle (2 miles).

Barnard Castle is a delightful old market town with broad streets and many 18th century stone houses, in a beautiful position on the steep north bank of the Tees. Charles Dickens stayed at the King's Head Hotel, in the Market Place, while investigating conditions in the Yorkshire schools (see Bowes, on Tour 6). Below the octagonal 18th century Market House is Blagroves House, a 16th century town mansion. The Castle (admission 9.30 to 4, to 5.30, or to 7, May-September; Sundays from 2), built by the Baliols after 1093, was confiscated in 1296 after the revolt of John Baliol, King of Scotland. The Bowes Museum (admission weekdays 10 to 4, 5 or 5.30, Sundays 2 to 4 or 5), east of the town, is a grandoise late-19th century mansion in the style of a French château, built for John Bowes and his Italian wife and now containing period rooms with outstanding collections of porcelain, furniture, paintings and ecclesiastical art. In the basement are rooms devoted to Teesdale rural life.

A67, recrossing the Tees, then B6277 (right) to Cotherstone (4 miles) and thence to Romaldkirk (2 miles).

Cotherstone, a characteristic stone village in a pleasant position south of the Tees, had a school of the 'Dotheboys Hall' type (see Bowes). Romaldkirk is a charming village scattered round a green, with grey sandstone houses and the interesting mother-church of Teesdale, of the 12th century and later and containing a remarkable 18th century pulpit and reading-desk.

B6277 on to Mickleton (2 miles) and thence, joining the road from Lunesdale (see below), to Middleton-in-Teesdale (2 miles).

Middleton-in-Teesdale is an agricultural and quarrying town (a former lead-mining centre), on the north bank of the river, surrounded by moorlands. B6277 goes on up the Tees for High Force ($4\frac{1}{2}$ miles), the most magnificent waterfall in England, where the foaming river throws itself over a sheer basalt cliff, more than 70 feet high, into a beautifully wooded glen.

B6277 back (south) from Middleton-in-Teesdale for 1 mile, then B6276 (right), ascending the long desolate Lunesdale for about $7\frac{1}{2}$ miles, then descending to join A66 $\frac{1}{2}$ mile east of Brough ($4\frac{1}{2}$ miles from the summit of the pass).

Brough. To reach this, the road crosses the watershed between the Lune, a tributary of the Tees, and the Eden at about 1550 feet. To the north extend the slopes of the remote and desolate Mickle Fell (2591 feet), the highest hill in Yorkshire. Brough is a former coaching station and market town on a tributary of the Eden, below the wilds of Stainmore Forest. The ruined Castle (admission 9.30 to 4, to 5.30, or to 7, May-September; Sundays from 2), to the south, stands within the Roman fort of Verterae. It was mostly built in the 12th century by Henry II, but has a keep partly restored by Lady Anne Clifford.

A66 on towards Warcop (3 miles; ½ mile to the left).

Warcop, on the Eden, has a church, mainly of the 13th and 15th centuries, containing floral crowns and crosses carried during the rushbearing festival on St. Peter's Day.

A66 on to Appleby (5 miles).

Appleby, an ancient royal borough, by long tradition the county town of Westmorland, is a market centre, making cheese, in the beautiful valley of the Eden, under the dark Pennine escarpment. The Parish Church, mostly of the 13th and 15th centuries, contains the 17th century monuments of the redoubtable Anne Clifford, Countess of Pembroke, and her mother. In the long Market Place is the 16th century Moot Hall, and from it Boroughgate, the fine main street, ascends steeply past St. Anne's Hospital, almshouses founded by the Lady Anne, to the castle at the top of the hill, long the seat of the Cliffords, which has a fine Norman keep, but was largely rebuilt in the 17th century.

B6260 south across the moors with distant views of the Lake District mountains, to Orton (10 miles) and thence to Tebay (2½ miles).

Orton is an old-world market village with a restored 13th and 15th century church which has a massive late-15th century tower. Tebay is a village on the Lune (the 'Lancashire' Lune) at the point where it begins to force a passage between the Howgill Fells, to the east, and the Shap Fells, which link the Pennines to the Lakeland fells.

A685 (right) down the valley of the Lune via Low Boroughbridge (2½ miles), then B6257 (left), hilly but interesting, and A684 (left again) across the river for Sedbergh (8½ miles).

Low Boroughbridge. Here are the earthworks of a Roman fort, beside the river. Sedbergh, finely situated on the Rawthey between the entrances to Garsdale and Dentdale (see below), and at the south foot of the steep Howgill Fells, is a stone-built market town famous for Sedbergh School, a public school founded in 1525 by Roger Lupton, Provost of Eton College and a native of the town. Some of the buildings are of the 18th century.

Unclassified road south (by the church), crossing the Rawthey and ascending Dentdale to Dent (5½ miles).

Dent, in the secluded green valley of the Dee and once famous for its knitters (of worsted stockings), is an old-world village with tortuous cobbled streets round which the colourful stone houses are huddled. The large church has 13th century nave arcades, but is otherwise of the 16th century. The upper part of the dale lies between the long moorland ridge of Rise Hill (1825 feet), to the north, and the prominent Whernside (2419 feet), the highest fell in the West Riding.

Unclassified road on through the upper reaches of Dentdale and ascending steeply to Newby Head (7 miles); then B6255 (left) down the long remote Widdale to Hawes (6½ miles).

Newby Head (1434 feet) is a farm on the watershed between the Widdale Beck, which flows north to Wensleydale, and the Gayle Beck, which descends south to Ribblesdale. Hawes is an old grey market town noted for its sheep sales and Wensleydale cheese.

A684 on through Hawes, then by an unclassified road left, crossing the Ure, then left again and right (from the road to Hardrow), before ascending steeply to the Buttertubs Pass (4 miles).

Hardrow is a hamlet near the foot of the ravine containing Hardrow Force, a waterfall about 90 feet high (the highest drop in Yorkshire), but impressive only after wet weather. The Buttertubs Pass (1726 feet), on the watershed between Wensleydale and Swaledale, takes its name from the Buttertubs, a series of deep fissures in the limestone, ½ mile on the north side of the pass, from which a wide view opens of Great Shunner Fell (2340 feet), to the west, and others of the wild Pennine hills.

Unclassified road on into the valley of the Muker Beck near Thwaite (2½ miles) then B6270 (right) to Muker (1 mile).

Thwaite is a pleasant hamlet at the south foot of the steep-sided hill of Kisdon (1636 feet), from which B6270 runs north to Keld (2 miles), a hamlet near several pretty waterfalls on the Swale. Muker, the former lead-mining capital of upper Swaledale, is a village of enchanting irregularity, with cottages of the dark Pennine gritstone. To the north the dale swings round the base of Kisdon towards Keld.

B6270 on down Swaledale to Gunnerside (3 miles) and thence to Reeth (6 miles), then across the river to Grinton (1 mile).

Swaledale is the narrowest, deepest, and most remote of the Yorkshire Dales, and in many ways the most fascinating. Gunnerside, Reeth and Grinton are described in Tour 4 (page 27).

B6270 on for 4½ miles, then A6108 continues through the dale, crossing the Swale to Richmond (5 miles), which is entered by Reeth Road and Victoria Road.

Marrick Priory. The road through this well-wooded section of Swaledale passes opposite the parish church of Marrick, which incorporates 12th century remains of Marrick Priory. Farther on, to the north, is Whitcliffe Scar, a limestone escarpment with a monument in memory of a horse that leapt over with its rider in 1606.

Tour 6
114miles

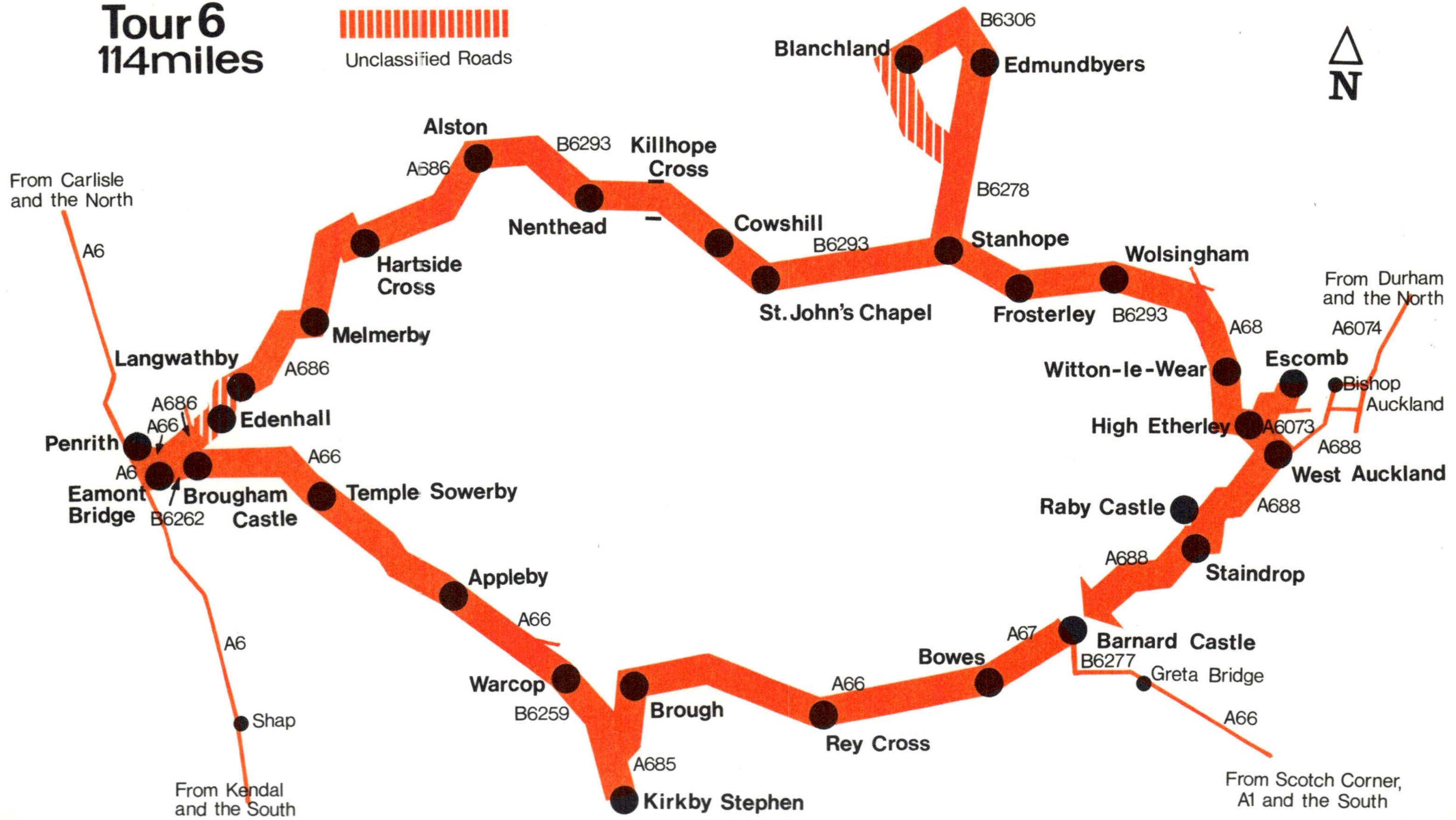

6. The Upper Pennines, with the Vale of Eden and Weardale

This tour, starting in County Durham, a little known and much maligned county, passes through the Stainmore Gap in the Pennines to the lovely Vale of Eden, which it descends all the way to Penrith. It then climbs steeply over one of the grandest stretches of the Pennine escarpment to the high-lying town of Alston, from which it re-enters Durham and runs through Weardale, where a detour may be taken to include Blanchland, a fascinating village just in Northumberland. Besides that of Barnard Castle itself, the tour takes in the interesting fortifications at Bowes, Brough, Brougham Castle and Raby Castle, as well as the old market towns of Kirkby Stephen, Appleby and Penrith.

Barnard Castle is described in Tour 5 (page 31).

A67 from Barnard Castle, crossing the Tees and ascending to Bowes (5 miles).

Bowes is a village in an exposed position on the east of the Pennine moorlands. Within the Roman fort of Lavatrae is the ruined keep of a Norman Castle (admission 9.30 to 4, to 5.30, or 7, May-September; Sundays from 2), built by Henry II to defend the Stainmore Gap (see below). At the west end of the village is a house supposed to be the original of 'Dotheboys Hall' in Dickens' *Nicholas Nickleby*.

A66 west, following a Roman forerunner, across the bleak moors of Stainmore Forest, then descending to Brough (13 miles).

The Stainmore Gap, which the road traverses, is one of the few breaches in the Pennine range; its summit level (1436 feet) is just west of Rey Cross, from which a wonderful view opens of the Eden valley with the Lakeland mountains beyond. Close by are the mounds of a Roman camp and part of the cross (of the 13th century or earlier) mentioned in Scott's 'Rokeby'. Brough is a former coaching station and market town on a tributary of the Eden, below the west slopes of the Forest. The ruined Castle (admission 9.30 to 4, to 5.30, or 7, May-September; Sundays from 2), to the south, stands within the Roman fort of Verterae. It was mostly built in the 12th century by Henry II, but has a keep partly restored by Lady Anne Clifford (see below).

A685 south into the Eden valley at Kirkby Stephen (4½ miles).

Kirkby Stephen is a pleasant old market town attractively situated on the river and noted for its Swaledale ram sale. It has a fine church of the 13th and 15th centuries, approached through a classical portico of 1810. To the south of the town opens Mallerstang, the wild green upper valley of the Eden, the road through which, between the long craggy escarpments of Mallerstang Edge (2328 feet), and Wild Boar Fell (2324 feet) leads to upper Wensleydale.

A685 back (north) and B6259 (left) through Warcop (5 miles).

Warcop, on the Eden, has a church, mainly of the 13th and 15th centuries, containing floral crowns and crosses carried during the rushbearing festival on St. Peter's Day.

A66 (left) to Appleby (5 miles).

Appleby, an ancient royal borough, by long tradition the county town of Westmorland, is a market centre, making cheese, in the beautiful valley of the Eden, under the dark Pennine escarpment. The Parish Church, mostly of the 13th and 15th centuries, contains the 17th century monuments of the redoubtable Anne Clifford, Countess of Pembroke, and her mother. In the long Market Place is the 16th century Moot Hall, and from it Boroughgate, the fine main street, ascends steeply past St. Anne's Hospital, almshouses founded by the Lady Anne, to the Castle at the top of the hill, long the seat of the Cliffords, which has a fine Norman keep, but was largely rebuilt in the 17th century.

A66 on down the Vale of Eden to Temple Sowerby ($6\frac{1}{2}$ miles) and thence to Brougham Castle (5 miles).

Temple Sowerby is an attractive village with red sandstone cottages below the abrupt Pennine escarpment. The Manor House, to the north, is a 16th and 18th century building. To the north-east rise the domed Cross Fell (2930 feet), the highest point on the Pennine range, and Great Dun Fell (2780 feet), with the prominent masts of a radar station. Brougham Castle (admission 9.30 to 4, to 5.30, or to 7, May-September; Sundays from 2), near the junction of the Lowther with the Eamont, adjoins the site of the Roman fort of Brocavum and has a 12th-13th century keep forming a single defence work with two gatehouses. Together with the chapel and other 13th-14th century buildings, it was restored by Lady Anne Clifford, who died here in 1675.

B6262, south of the castle, to Eamont Bridge (1 mile).

Eamont Bridge. Here, beside the road from the castle, is St. Wilfrid's Chapel, built in 1658 (one of the few churches built in the Commonwealth period) and restored about 1850, when the Continental woodwork and stained glass were introduced. The Ullswater road runs west between King Arthur's Round Table, on the south, and Mayburgh, two Neolithic earthworks that were probably sacred sites.

A6 right, crossing the Lowther and the Eamont, to Penrith ($1\frac{1}{2}$ miles).

Penrith is an old market town with narrow congested streets and many 16th-18th century houses. In the churchyard of St. Andrew's (1722) are three weathered crosses and four carved gravestones, all perhaps of the 10th century. In a park near the station, to the west, is the late-14th century Castle (admission daily), altered by Richard III when he was Duke of Gloucester and Lord Warden of the Western Marches, and dismantled during the Civil War. Penrith Beacon (937 feet), to the north-east of the town, commands a fine view of the Pennines, Helvellyn and other Lakeland fells.

A6 back (south) and A66 (left) to Carleton (1 mile), then A686 (left again) for 1½ miles and by an unclassified road (right) to Edenhall (1½ miles more) then on to rejoin A686 and cross the Eden to Langwathby (1 mile).

Edenhall has a much-Gothicized 14th century church with 17th century armorial glass and memorials of the Musgraves, who lived at the now-demolished hall. Langwathby, built in characteristic fashion round a green, has a church containing 17th century armour of the local militia. The early-prehistoric stone circle known as Long Meg and her Daughters is over 2 miles north, beyond Little Salkeld.

A686 on to Melmerby (4 miles) and then, ascending steeply, with many twists and turns, up the long Pennine escarpment to Hartside Cross (4½ miles).

Melmerby is a pleasant village scattered round a large green, backed by the steep moorland escarpment of the Pennines, which rises to Melmerby Fell (2331 feet). Hartside Cross, on the very edge of the escarpment, commands the most exhilarating prospect over the Vale of Eden to the distant Lakeland fells.

A686 on, descending over the heather-clad moorlands, into South Tynedale, for Alston (6 miles).

Alston, on a slope above the dale, surrounded by wild green fells, is an agricultural town and a former lead-mining centre, with steep cobbled streets and a restored 18th century market cross in the highest market place in England (except for that at Buxton, in Derbyshire).

B6293 east into the valley of the Nent for Nenthead (5 miles), then ascending steeply to Killhope Cross (1 mile).

Nenthead, above the upper reaches of the river, with fluorspar-processing works, is one of the highest villages in England (1415 feet). Killhope Cross, which affords extensive views over the swelling moorlands stretching north to the Allendales and south-west towards Cross Fell, is the highest point reached by any main road in England (2056 feet).

B6293 descends into the upper part of Weardale at Cowshill (4 miles), then follows the Wear down to St. John's Chapel (3 miles) and thence to Stanhope (6½ miles).

St. John's Chapel is an attractive village engaged in agriculture and quarrying, in the pastoral upper section of the dale. Stanhope, an old town with a 13th century church, is the capital of upper Weardale, and the centre of a quarrying district with cement works and lead mines. Near the Heathery Burn, to the east, is a limestone cave in which the tools of Bronze Age metal workers were discovered.

B6278, climbing steeply on the north side of the dale, ascends for 3 miles over the heather-covered moors of Muggleswick Common, where an unclassified road branches left to descend towards Blanchland (3 miles more). Stanhope may be regained via B6306 and Edmundbyers ($4\frac{1}{2}$ miles), a typical moorside village with a green, and thence by B6278, recrossing the moors, a detour of 21 miles in all.

Blanchland is an enchanting village in the sequestered upper valley of the Derwent. Remains of a 12th century abbey are preserved in the church and built into the planned village, whose unusual square is entered through the abbey gateway, of about 1500. The charming stone houses were built soon after 1752, when also the Lord Crewe Arms was formed out of 13th century ruins, probably of the abbey guest house.

B6293 on through Weardale to Frosterley ($2\frac{1}{2}$ miles) and thence to Wolsingham ($3\frac{1}{2}$ miles).

Frosterley is a village long noted for its marble, a black limestone rich in fossils. Wolsingham is a small town at the entrance to the upper part of Weardale, with many 16th-18th century houses.

B6293 on for 4 miles, then A68 (right) to Witton-le-Wear (3 miles more).

Witton-le-Wear is a village attractively situated above the north bank of the river, with a medieval tower-house remodelled in the 17th century. Witton Castle, in a fine park (admission daily in summer) on the south side of the Wear, is a 15th century tower-house extended and altered in the 18th and 19th centuries.

A68 on to High Etherley (3 miles) and thence to West Auckland ($1\frac{1}{2}$ miles). From A6073, running east from High Etherley towards Bishop Auckland, a side road descends to Escomb ($2\frac{1}{2}$ miles).

Escomb is a village (now being rebuilt) on the Wear, with a complete Saxon church, probably of the 7th century and certainly one of the earliest in England, now judiciously restored, with new furnishings, by Sir Albert Richardson. West Auckland is a characteristic village with 17th century houses round a large green, on the edge of the Durham coalfield.

A688 south-west, passing Raby Castle (see below), to Staindrop (5 miles) and thence to Barnard Castle (6 miles).

Staindrop is an attractive village with a long tree-shaded green. The interesting church shows work from the Saxon period to the 15th century and contains splendid 15th century and later monuments of the Nevilles. Raby Castle (admission Easter and May-September, Wednesdays, Saturdays and Bank Holidays, 2 to 5; each weekday in the late summer Bank Holiday week), nearly 1 mile north, the seat of the Nevilles and since 1626 of the Vanes, is one of the largest and most magnificent 14th century castles in England, partly remodelled in the mid-19th century and containing many fine English and other paintings.

7. The Roman Wall, the Upper Pennines and Tynedale

This tour follows the course of the great wall of Hadrian, built from the Tyne to the Solway Firth. The Wall is not only of supreme antiquarian interest, but traverses some wild and beautiful country, crossing the lovely North Tynedale at Chollerford and at Gilsland reaching the Irthing valley. The tour leaves the Wall near the charming Lanercost Priory (beyond which there is little of it to see) and from the market town of Brampton it turns towards South Tynedale, which it ascends as far as Alston. An exhilarating road crosses the moors and the wooded Allendale to reach the South Tyne again, and the Tyne is followed past the market town of Hexham, which has a priory church full of interest, and the charming village of Corbridge, near a large Roman garrison town.

From Newcastle upon Tyne by Westgate Road and A69 to Benwell (2 miles) and thence to Heddon-on-the-Wall ($5\frac{1}{2}$ miles).

Hadrian's Wall. The first part of this tour, between Newcastle and Banks (near Lanercost), follows the course of this great fortification built in A.D. 122-30 under the orders of the Emperor Hadrian as the frontier of the Roman province of Britain, and stretching right across country from Wallsend, on the Tyne, to Bowness-on-Solway, a distance of over 73 miles. The wall itself, built of stone, stood about 15 feet high and varies from $7\frac{1}{2}$ to 9 feet thick. On its north side, for most of its course, it is followed by a ditch about 27 feet wide, and to the south, at a short but varying distance, is the Vallum, a flat-bottomed ditch 20 feet wide at the top, running between earth mounds and intended to protect the fortification on that side. The wall was patrolled from so-called 'milecastles,' small barrack buildings about 1620 yards apart, and between these were two smaller turrets at equal spaces. The Roman garrison were quartered in 17 large forts of rectangular shape, some of which were built slightly later than the wall and replaced an earlier series of forts along the Stanegate, a road farther south, parallel to the Tyne. The finest remaining sections of the Wall are near Chollerford and between Sewingshields and Birdoswald; the most interesting forts are those at Chesters (near Chollerford) and Housesteads. From Newcastle to Sewingshields the remains of the wall were used as a foundation for the Military Road to Carlisle, built after the Jacobite rising of 1745 (when the Hanoverian troops were unable to get across country and come to grips with Prince Charles Edward Stuart), and in consequence there is little of the wall itself to be seen. The ditch and vallum, however, are distinctive for most of their course beyond the suburbs of Newcastle. At Benwell, in a residential estate, are remains of a small temple that stood outside the Roman fort of Condercum. At Heddon-on-the-Wall practically the first upstanding lengths of the wall can be seen, and the village has an interesting church of the 12th and 13th centuries.

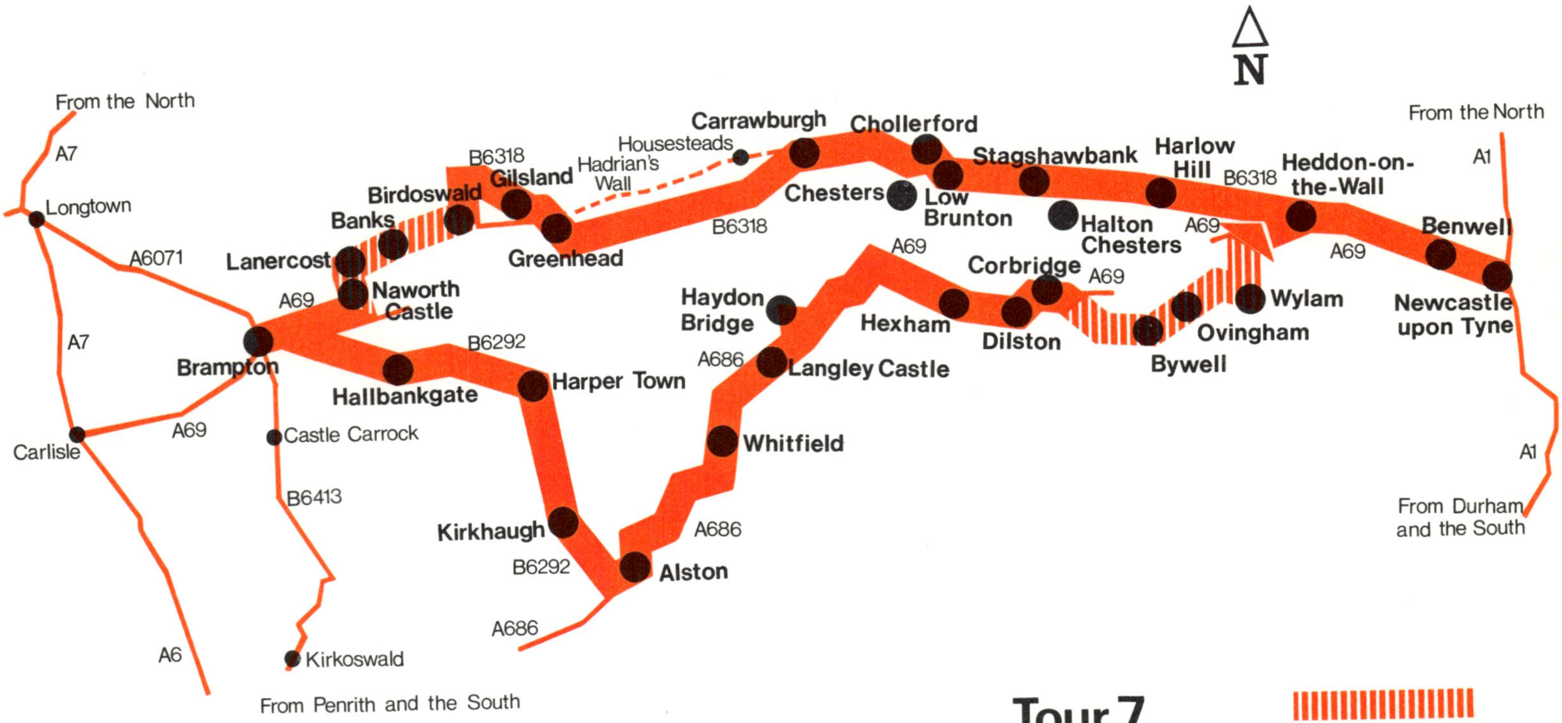

Tour 7
115miles

B6318, following the Military Road (see above), to Harlow Hill (3½ miles) and thence to Halton Chesters (5½ miles), ½ mile beyond which is Stagshawbank.

Halton Chesters. Here are the extensive earthworks of the fort of Onnum, and at Halton, ½ mile south, is a 14th century pele-tower of typical Border type. Stagshawbank, an open common long famous for the large sheep fair held here, is at the point where the Wall was penetrated by Dere Street, the Roman road that led from the supply-base of Corstopitum (see Corbridge, page 44) into Scotland.

B6318 on to St. Oswald's (3 miles) and thence to Low Brunton (1 mile).

St. Oswald's is a solitary 18th century chapel in a lonely position just north of the Wall, marking the place where St. Oswald, King of Northumbria, pitched his camp before the great battle of A.D. 634 in which he defeated the heathen King Cadwalla. At Low Brunton the road up North Tynedale cuts through the line of Hadrian's Wall. To the south is a fine stretch of the wall, with an excellent example of a turret.

B6318 on over the North Tyne to Chollerford (½ mile) and thence to Chesters (½ mile), on the left.

Chollerford is in a delightful pastoral and wooded valley, and here the river is crossed by a late-18th century bridge. Chesters has a fine park containing the extensive remains of the Roman cavalry fort of Cilurnum (admission weekdays 9 or 9.30 to 4, 5 or 5.30; Sundays, 2 to 4 or 4.30), which stood on the Wall. Near the west bank of the North Tyne is the large and well-preserved bath-house, the finest in Britain. When the river is low, two piers of a Roman bridge are revealed, and on the farther bank is part of the east abutment. The Museum in the park contains an outstanding collection of antiquities from the Wall.

B6318, ascending out of the valley to Limestone Corner (3 miles) and going on thence to Carrawburgh (1½ miles).

Limestone Corner (823 feet), where the Vallum and ditch are cut through the solid rock, affords a wide view north over North Tyne-dale to the Simonside and Cheviot Hills. Beyond the farm of Carrawburgh are the earthworks of the fort of Brocolitia, and outside these are the remarkable remains of a Temple of Mithras, of the 3rd century, excavated since 1950.

B6318 on towards Sewingshields (2 miles) and then south of the Wall for Housesteads (2½ miles).

Sewingshields. Before reaching this farm, both the Military Road and the Vallum diverge south from the line of Hadrian's Wall, which climbs along the crest of the Great Whin Sill, a long escarpment of basaltic crags, commanding a wild view over the Northumbrian moors to the Border hills. Housesteads, nearly ½ mile north of the road by a footpath, stands on the edge of the Whin Sill. The well-preserved remains (admission daily 9.30 to 4, to 5.30, or to 7, May-September; Sundays from 2 in winter) of the infantry fort of Vercovicium (or Borcovicium) are the most interesting and the finest in position of all the forts on the Wall. A Museum near the farm contains models and plans, as well as finds made in the neighbourhood. Beyond the wall are the Northumberland Lakes, in a moorland setting of extreme desolation. To the west of Housesteads is a fine example of a Milecastle, and it is worth following the wall on foot over Hotbank Crags to the sheer rock wall above the charmingly situated Crag Lough, a distance of about 1½ miles.

B6318 on to the Twice Brewed Inn (2½ miles) and thence to Greenhead (6 miles).

The Twice Brewed Inn is in a very solitary position. To the north-west rises Winshields Crag (1230 feet), part of the Great Whin Sill, where Hadrian's Wall reaches its greatest height. The far-reaching view in clear weather includes the Scottish hills to the north and north-west, Cross Fell on the Pennines to the south, and Saddleback and Skiddaw, in the Lake District, to the south-west. To the west, the Wall is less well preserved, though a good section can be seen where it traverses the line of basalt crags known as the Nine Nicks of Thirlwall. Greenhead is on a tributary of the South Tyne at the junction of the Military Road with the main Newcastle-Carlisle road.

B6318 (right) through Gilsland (2 miles), then by an unclassified road (left) to Birdoswald (2 miles).

Gilsland is a former small spa and an angling resort in the pleasant Irthing valley, described in *Guy Mannering* by Sir Walter Scott, who first met his future wife here, in 1797. A section of Hadrian's Wall has been exposed to the west, in the garden of the old vicarage, and another fine stretch descends to the farm of Willowford, beyond which can be seen the abutment of the Bridge by which the Wall crossed the Irthing. On the bank beyond is a Milecastle, from which the Wall goes on to Birdoswald, a farm adjoining the fort of Camboglanna (admission daily, on application), one of the largest forts on the Wall, though not one of the best preserved. On the bleak moors stretching to the north can be seen the huge Rocket Testing Establishment at Spadeadam. To the west of Birdoswald, the Wall was first constructed of turf (to be rebuilt in stone later in the 1st century) and some remains of the turf wall can still be seen. To the east of the hamlet of Banks is a fine example of a turret, but beyond this, as far as the Solway Firth, very little of the Wall is now to be seen.

Unclassified road on, north of the Irthing, to Banks (3 miles), then left, leaving the line of the Wall, to Lanercost (1 mile).

Lanercost is charmingly situated beside the Irthing, which is crossed by a striking medieval bridge. The Priory (admission 9.30

to 4, to 5.30, or to 7, May-September; Sundays from 2) was founded in the 12th century for Augustinian canons. The nave, used since 1740 as the parish church, is an exquisite example of Early English architecture, but the 13th century choir and transepts, which contain tombs of the Dacres of Naworth, are in ruins, as are most of the claustral buildings.

Unclassified road over the Irthing (see above) and left, passing Naworth Castle (1 mile); then A69 (right) to Brampton (3 miles).

Naworth Castle, in a beautiful park, was built in the 14th century and passed in 1577 from the Dacres to 'Belted Will Howard' (who has been misrepresented by Scott in *The Lay of the Last Minstrel*). He made considerable alterations, and the castle was well-restored after a fire in 1844. Brampton is an old-world red-sandstone market town with an octagonal Moot Hall of 1817 in the cobbled Market Place. The church, built in 1878 by Philip Webb (and his only church), has windows full of richly-coloured glass by William Morris and Burne-Jones.

A69 back (east) to The Sands, then B6292 (right) to Hallbankgate (3½ miles) and traversing the northern foot of the Pennine moorlands as they fall steeply towards the Tyne Gap. At the hamlet of Harper Town (6 miles) the road reaches the secluded South Tynedale, which it ascends past Kirkhaugh (6 miles), then joins A686 and crosses the river to Alston (3 miles).

Kirkhaugh is a scattered hamlet to the south of which, on the edge of the moors, are the distinctive ramparts of Whitley Castle, a Roman fort of unknown name. Alston is described in Tour 6 (page 37).

A686 north, on the east slopes of South Tynedale, then across the moors, crossing the Northumberland boundary at over 1500 feet, before descending at length into the lovely wooded valley of the West Allen, which it reaches at Whitfield (9 miles). The road goes on down the valley and crosses the Allen below the junction of its two branches, from which it climbs in great zigzags on to the heights again and then drops down steadily past Langley Castle (6 miles) to reach the South Tyne at Haydon Bridge (1½ miles). This road from Alston to Haydon Bridge is one of the most beautiful in England.

Langley Castle (admission May-September, Wednesday, 2 to 7; or on written application), in a charming valley, is an impressive 14th century Border pele-tower, well restored and now used as a school. Haydon Bridge is a small town on both banks of the South Tyne, which is crossed by a long bridge.

A69 on south of the river, with charming views, to Hexham (7 miles).

Hexham is a delightful agricultural town with a long main street. To the east of the Market Place is the 14th century Moot Hall (now a library; admission Monday and Wednesday 6 to 8; Wednesdays also 2.30 to 4.30), the tower house of the bailiff of the

Archbishop of York, who was lord of the regality of Hexham; and farther east is the Manor Office of 1332, the medieval prison of the regality, the only one in England. The cathedral-like Priory Church retains the original crypt of the 7th century church built by St. Wilfrid. The Norman nave, destroyed by the Scots in 1296, was rebuilt in 1908, but the magnificent choir and the transepts, with their unique and well-worn night stairs leading from the canons' dormitory, are mainly of the 12th and 13th centuries. In the south transept are a Roman monument and a Saxon cross, and the choir is full of interesting features, including a Saxon bishop's stone chair, 15th century chantry chapels, and numerous paintings on the rood-screen and elsewhere.

A69 on south of the Tyne to Dilston (2½ miles; on the right).

Dilston has a ruined 15th century Castle, the home of the last Earl of Derwentwater, executed for his part in the Jacobite rising of 1715.

A69 on over the Tyne to Corbridge (1 mile).

Corbridge, a large and interesting village on the north bank of the stony Tyne, was once the capital of the Saxon Northumbria. The church, mostly of the 13th century, has a unique Saxon porch-tower with a Roman arch, and at the edge of the churchyard is a 14th century fortified Vicarage of a type peculiar to Northumberland. To the west, north of the river, are the extensive remains of Corstopitum (admission daily 9.30 to 4, to 5.30, or to 7, May-September; Sundays in winter from 2), an important garrison town and a supply-depot serving the legions on Hadrian's Wall. The excavated buildings include a huge storehouse, one of the largest Roman buildings discovered in Britain; and the Museum contains a fine collection of inscribed and sculptured stones.

A69 on, north of the Tyne, for 1½ miles, then by an unclassified road (right) to Bywell (3 miles).

Bywell, attractively situated on the river, is a 'decayed' village with a 15th century gatehouse-tower and two churches in adjacent churchyards, both mainly of the 13th century, though one has a fine Saxon tower.

Unclassified road beside the Tyne to Ovingham (2½ miles) and thence to Wylam (2 miles).

Ovingham has another 13th century church with a Saxon tower, near the foot of which is the grave of Thomas Bewick, the famous engraver. Prudhoe, on the steep opposite bank of the river, has a castle of the 12th-14th centuries. Beside the railway east of Wylam is the cottage birthplace (1781) of George Stephenson, the locomotive engineer.

Unclassified road north, away from the Tyne, for 1 mile, then A69 (right) to Heddon-on-the-Wall (1½ miles) and thence to Newcastle upon Tyne (7½ miles).

8. The Lake District, including Derwentwater and Ullswater

The last three tours in the book cover the mountainous Lake District, in the opinion of many travellers the loveliest and most satisfying part of England. The routes cross and re-cross at various points, and inevitably overlap to some extent, because of the scarcity of good roads, but no one will mind seeing any of the lakes and dales twice or more. This tour, starting from Windermere 'Village', includes no less than nine of the lakes. It also takes in the fascinating old towns of Ambleside, Keswick and Penrith, and the villages of Troutbeck and Grasmere (the home of William Wordsworth), and runs through the beautiful valleys of Borrowdale and Patterdale and over the wild passes of Honister and Kirkstone.

Windermere Village (usually so called to distinguish it from the lake) is a small slate-built town that grew up only after the building in 1847 of the railway, against which Wordsworth protested vigorously in a sonnet. Although the town stands some 300 feet above the lake, it affords hardly any views of the Lakeland mountains or even of Windermere itself. Much the most comprehensive view is obtained from Orrest Head (784 feet), reached in about 20 minutes by footpath from the station. Practically the whole of the lake is in view, and a mountain indicator points out the Lakeland fells, most of which can be seen.

From Windermere by A591 to Troutbeck Bridge (1 mile) and thence to Low Wood (2 miles).

Windermere. Beyond the hamlet of Troutbeck Bridge the road skirts the north-east shore of this, the largest lake in England, 10½ miles long, though nowhere more than 1¼ miles wide. Its name, of Norse origin, signifies the lake of Vinand, not the 'winding lake'. (As the suffix 'mere' means 'lake', the term Lake Windermere, often met with, is an unnecessary duplication.) The shores of the lake are thickly and charmingly wooded; the fells in the neighbourhood, if not particularly high, are everywhere rocky and colourful, and the head of the lake is enclosed by a girdle of imposing mountains. Low Wood, a hotel on the lake shore favoured by honeymoon couples, commands one of the loveliest views in Lakeland, the fells from the Coniston Old Man to Bowfell and the Langdale Pikes being especially well seen.

A591 on to Waterhead (1 mile).

Waterhead, at the north end of Windermere, is the terminus of the steamers which ply on the lake in summer from Bowness (see Tour 9) and Lake Side (near Newby Bridge). To the west is Borrans Park, with a bathing place and a fine view down the lake, and next to this is the Borrans Field, with some remains of the small Roman fort of Galava.

On A591, leaving Windermere, to Ambleside (½ mile).

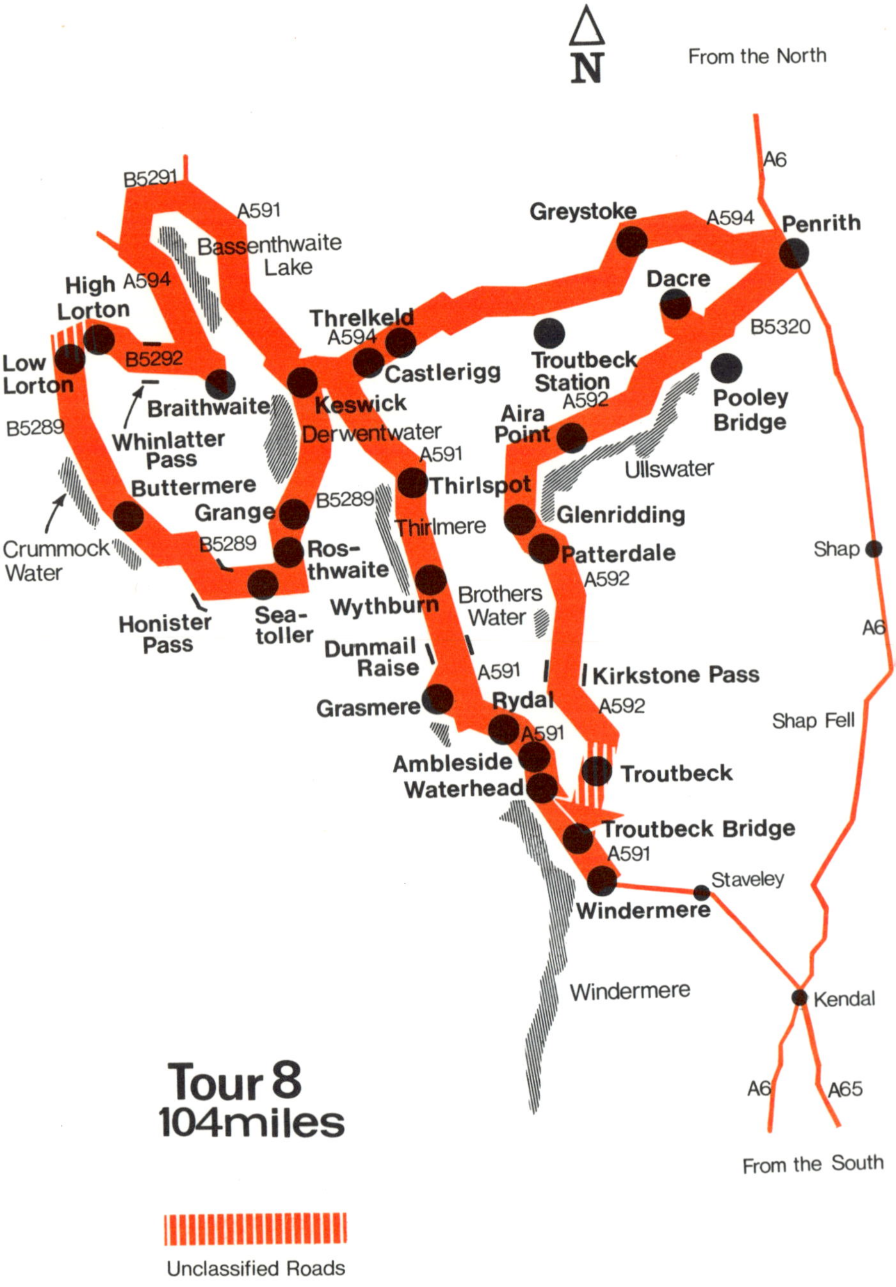

Tour 8
104miles

Ambleside, one of the most popular resorts in the Lake District, is a thriving town built of the local slate-stone and delightfully situated in the verdant vale of the Rothay. The Stock Beck, which hurries through on its way to join the Rothay, is spanned by the 17th century Old Bridge House, a tiny garden house, now a National Trust information centre. St. Mary's Church, built by Sir Gilbert Scott in 1854, has a prominent spire and a memorial chapel to William Wordsworth and his family, and a large mural depicts the rush-bearing festival held annually in late-July. The Stock Gill Force is a charming waterfall reached by the lane from the Salutation Hotel.

A591 on through the Rothay valley to Rydal (1½ miles).

Rydal is a colourful hamlet with Rydal Mount (above the church), where William Wordsworth died in 1850, and Dora's Field, bought by the poet and noted for its daffodils. It stands at the foot of Rydal Water, a delectable small lake between the precipice of Nab Scar, on the north, and the rugged Loughrigg Fell. Beyond the white Nab Cottage, where Thomas De Quincey lived in 1816, the road rounds a sharp promontory to reveal a sudden view of Grasmere, one of the most charming of the lakes, though hardly a mile long, beyond which rises Helm Crag, remarkable for the jumbled crags on its summit ridge. At Town End, a hamlet at the north-east angle of the lake, is Dove Cottage (admission March to mid-January, weekdays, 10 to 4.30 or 6), a typical Lakeland dwelling, the home from 1799 of Wordsworth and his sister Dorothy. Close by is an interesting Wordsworth Museum (admission Easter-October only, weekdays, 10 to 6).

A591 alongside the shores of Rydal Water and Grasmere, to Grasmere village (2½ miles).

Grasmere, a village with characteristic slate-built houses, lies west of the main Keswick road and has a rustic church, partly of the 14th century. In the churchyard, beside the murmuring Rothay, are the graves of William Wordsworth, his wife and his sister. The Wordsworths moved in 1808 to Allan Bank, ¼ mile north-west, and in 1811 to the Parsonage, opposite the church, which they left in 1813 for Rydal. A rush-bearing service is held in the church on the Saturday nearest 6th August; and the famous Grasmere Sports (first held in 1852) take place on the Thursday nearest 20th August).

A591 up the Vale of Rothay to Dunmail Raise (3 miles) descending thence to Wythburn (1 mile), on Thirlmere.

Dunmail Raise is described in Tour 10 (page 62). Wythburn is a hamlet with a tiny 17th century church near the south end of Thirlmere, a lake that was converted in 1879 into a reservoir for Manchester, which is supplied by an aqueduct nearly 100 miles long. The level was raised 50 feet by a great dam at the north end, crossed by the road connecting the main road with the quieter road on the west shore, but the lake is now enclosed by thick pine plantations, restricting the views.

A591 along the east side of Thirlmere, under the steep slopes of Helvellyn, to Thirlspot ($3\frac{1}{2}$ miles), near the north end, then on, away from the Vale of St. John, for Keswick (5 miles).

Keswick is described in Tour 10 (page 61).

B5289 to the Lodore Hotel (3 miles) and thence to Grange-in-Borrowdale ($1\frac{1}{2}$ miles).

Derwentwater. Beyond Castle Head (see page 61) the road skirts the east shore of this, the loveliest of all the lakes, its surface dotted with wooded islands, and its shores a satisfying blend of rich woodland, steep crag, and rugged green fell. In a ravine behind the Lodore Hotel, beyond the south-east angle of the lake, are the famous Lodore Falls, praised by Southey, but imposing only after heavy rain. Grange is a charming village at the entrance to the 'Jaws of Borrowdale' and at the beginning of the quieter road round the west side of Derwentwater.

B5289 through Borrowdale to Rosthwaite ($1\frac{1}{2}$ miles) and thence to Seatoller (1 mile).

Borrowdale, through which the road runs beyond Grange, is the valley of the Derwent and the most beautiful dale in Lakeland, narrow and densely wooded at first, between Grange Fell, at the foot of which is the Bowder Stone, a huge mass of rock balanced on its edge, and the distinctive Castle Crag, a steep cone of rock apparently filling the dale. Before reaching Rosthwaite, the dale opens out to a level green strath enclosed by verdant and craggy fells, extending beyond Seatoller, a hamlet on a steep slope above the dale, which continues south to Seathwaite Farm, the wettest inhabited place in England, enclosed by lofty heights.

B5289 climbs steeply to the Honister Pass ($1\frac{1}{2}$ miles), then descends at length to Gatesgarth ($2\frac{1}{2}$ miles), beyond which it skirts the north shore of Buttermere to reach Buttermere village ($1\frac{1}{2}$ miles).

The Honister Pass, which commands a fine retrospect of Borrowdale, with Helvellyn beyond, is the wildest road pass in Lakeland. Above Honister Hause (1176 feet), the summit, rises the sheer face of Honister Crag, scarred by huge slate quarries. The road descends through a savage defile to the farm of Gatesgarth, at the head of a valley, overshadowed by the precipitous Fleetwith Pike. Beyond the farm it runs alongside Buttermere, one of the most delectable of the lakes, though only $1\frac{1}{4}$ miles long, filling the bottom of a trough-like valley on whose south side rise the steep flanks of High Stile and Red Pike. The charming Buttermere village is on the level strath between the lake and Crummock Water, at the foot of the abrupt Newlands Hause.

B5289 on along the east side of Crummock Water and thence through the Vale of Lorton to Low Lorton (6 miles).

Crummock Water is an attractive lake, $2\frac{1}{2}$ miles long, below the soaring west slopes of the bulky Grasmoor group. The best viewpoint is the sharp promontory of Hause Point, where the road crosses a rib of rock below Rannerdale Knott. At Low Lorton, in the pleasant vale of the Cocker, is Lorton Hall (admission Bank Holidays, 2 to 6; or by appointment), a medieval pele-tower with 17th century additions.

Unclassified road (right) to High Lorton (½ mile), then B5292 over the Whinlatter Pass (2½ miles), descending to Braithwaite (3½ miles).

Thornthwaite Forest, on either side of the Whinlatter Pass (1043 feet), was one of the earliest plantations of the Forestry Commission, and now extends south towards the top of Grizedale Pike and east to the shores of Bassenthwaite Lake.

A594 north along the west shore of Bassenthwaite Lake to the Pheasant Inn (4½ miles), then B5291 (left) round the foot of the lake for 1½ miles and A591 (right) on the east side of the lake for Keswick (8½ miles).

Bassenthwaite Lake, nearly 4 miles long, is the only 'Lake' described as such in the Lake District. Its west shore commands a fine view of Skiddaw and its satellites. From the charming old Pheasant Inn the road crosses the Ouse Bridge over the Derwent and skirts the pleasant grounds of Armathwaite Hall (now a hotel), which afford a fine view up the lake. The road on the east shore traverses the base of the Skiddaw fells, then crosses the level Vale of Keswick. Crosthwaite church, to the right of the road (½ mile from Keswick), is mainly of the 14th and 16th centuries and has a monument (with an inscription by Wordsworth) to Robert Southey, whose grave is in the churchyard.

A594 east up the valley of the Greta for 1 mile, then by an unclassified road (right) ascending past Castlerigg (1 mile) and rejoining A594 farther on for Threlkeld (2 miles).

Castlerigg, an early-prehistoric stone circle, stands on a ridge commanding magnificent views of Skiddaw and Saddleback. Threlkeld, finely situated at the foot of the massive buttresses of Saddleback, or Blencathra (2847 feet), has the kennels of the Blencathra Foxhounds and a memorial in the churchyard to 45 "noted veterans of the chase", most of whom are buried here.

A594 on to Troutbeck Station (4½ miles)—from which A5091 runs south direct to Aira Point (5 miles; see below)—and thence to Greystoke (4½ miles) and on to Penrith (5½ miles).

Greystoke. The road traverses the southern base of Saddleback, then crosses an open upland to this well-kept village whose interesting 13th-15th century church has much medieval glass. The Castle, mostly of the 17th and 19th centuries, was the seat of the Howard family for 400 years. Penrith is described in Tour 6.

B5320 south-west to the Eamont, which it follows past Dalemain (3 miles) to the foot of Ullswater near Pooley Bridge (2 miles).

Dalemain is a house of the 15th or 16th century with a graceful front of about 1740. A road on the right a mile farther on leads to Dacre (1 mile more), which has a massive Castle of the early 14th century. For Pooley Bridge, see Tour 9.

A592 along the north shore of Ullswater to Aira Point (5 miles; see above) and thence to Glenridding ($2\frac{1}{2}$ miles).

Ullswater is the second in size among the English lakes ($7\frac{1}{2}$ miles long) and is the grandest in scenery. It consists of three distinct reaches, and the upper reach, surrounded by the fells and crags of the Helvellyn and Fairfield ranges, is particularly splendid. The road, with beautiful views throughout, runs below Gowbarrow Park, over which roam red and fallow deer, and crosses the Aira Beck, which $\frac{1}{2}$ mile upstream throws itself over Aira Force, a fall 65 feet high in a deep winding ravine. The road runs under Glencoyne Wood before reaching Glenridding, a village near the head of the lake and the terminus of the motor-yacht service from Pooley Bridge.

A592 on to Patterdale (1 mile) and thence past Brothers Water (2 miles) before ascending steeply to the summit of the Kirkstone Pass ($3\frac{1}{2}$ miles).

Patterdale is a village in the charming dale of the same name, about $\frac{1}{2}$ mile above the head of Ullswater and near the entrance to Grisedale, which penetrates deep into the heart of the Helvellyn range. From Brothers Water, a small lake near the foot of the beautiful Dovedale, with its fine upstanding crags, the road is steep and winding (and very busy in summer) up to the top of the Kirkstone Pass (1489 feet), where the solitary inn is the fifth highest licensed house in England. A steep road descends direct from the inn to Ambleside.

A592 on for 3 miles to reach the Troutbeck valley, then unclassified road (right) to Troutbeck (1 mile). This road affords many attractive glimpses of Windermere.

Troutbeck is a charming village embowered in orchards and stretched out along the hillside above its valley. The Mortal Man Inn, partly of the 17th century, at the north end, has a sign painted by J. C. Ibbetson. Townend (admission every Wednesday, also daily except Monday and Saturday from Easter to September, 2 to 6 or dusk), at the south end, is a characteristic 17th century yeoman's house with carved woodwork and furniture.

Unclassified road on, descending to Troutbeck Bridge ($1\frac{1}{2}$ miles); then A591 (left) to Windermere Village (1 mile).

9. The Lake District, including Coniston Water and Ullswater

This tour, like Tour 8 and Tour 10, runs through the Lake District, but it includes also the little-visited country between Lakeland and Morecambe Bay. Some five of the lakes can be seen, and the tour also takes in the interesting market town of Kendal, the seaside resort of Grange-over-Sands and the popular lakeside resort of Bowness-on-Windermere. En route are the charming villages of Coniston, Hawkshead and Askham, the varied houses of Sizergh Castle, Levens Hall and Holker Hall, and not least the beautiful monastic remains of Furness Abbey and the priory church at Cartmel.

Kendal, the administrative headquarters of Westmorland and the southern 'gateway' to the Lake District, is an old-world market town in the vale of the Kent, and has long been famous for its manufacture of woollen cloth. A feature of the town are the many narrow 'yards' or alleys, supposed to have been built so that the townsfolk could protect themselves against Scottish raiders. In Redmayne's Yard, off Highgate, the main street, is the cottage in which George Romney, the artist, lived as a young man. Abbot Hall (admission weekdays, except Thursday, 10.30 to 5.30; Sundays, 2.30 to 5.30), near Kirkland, to the south, is a charming 18th century house, now a fine art gallery and craft museum. The restored Parish Church, mainly of the 13th and 15th centuries, is remarkable for the number of its chapels and its full-length double aisles. Beyond the Nether Bridge is the house in which Romney died in 1802. In Stricklandgate, the north continuation of Highgate is the house in which Prince Charles Edward Stuart lodged in 1745-6 on his journeys both south and north. To the east of the river are the Borough Museum (admission weekdays, 10 to 4 or 5), with good collections of geology and local history, and the 13th-14th century ruins of the Castle, where Catherine Parr, the last queen of Henry VIII, was born.

From Kendal by Kirkland, Milnthorpe Road and A6 to Sizergh Castle (3½ miles) and thence to Levens Bridge (1½ miles).

Sizergh Castle (admission April-September, Wednesdays, 2 to 5.45), the home of the Strickland family since the 13th century, consists of a well-preserved 14th century pele-tower, with Tudor additions and containing Stuart relics. Levens Hall (admission May to mid-September, Tuesdays, Wednesdays, Thursdays and Sundays, 2 to 5; gardens daily, 10 to 5.30), just beyond Levens Bridge, is an Elizabethan house incorporating a 13th century pele-tower, in a fascinating topiary garden laid out in the 17th century.

A590 west, crossing the Gilpin at the foot of the Lyth Valley, and under the sheer limestone crag of Whitbarrow Scar to Lindale (6½ miles); then B5277 (left) to Grange-over-Sands (1½ miles).

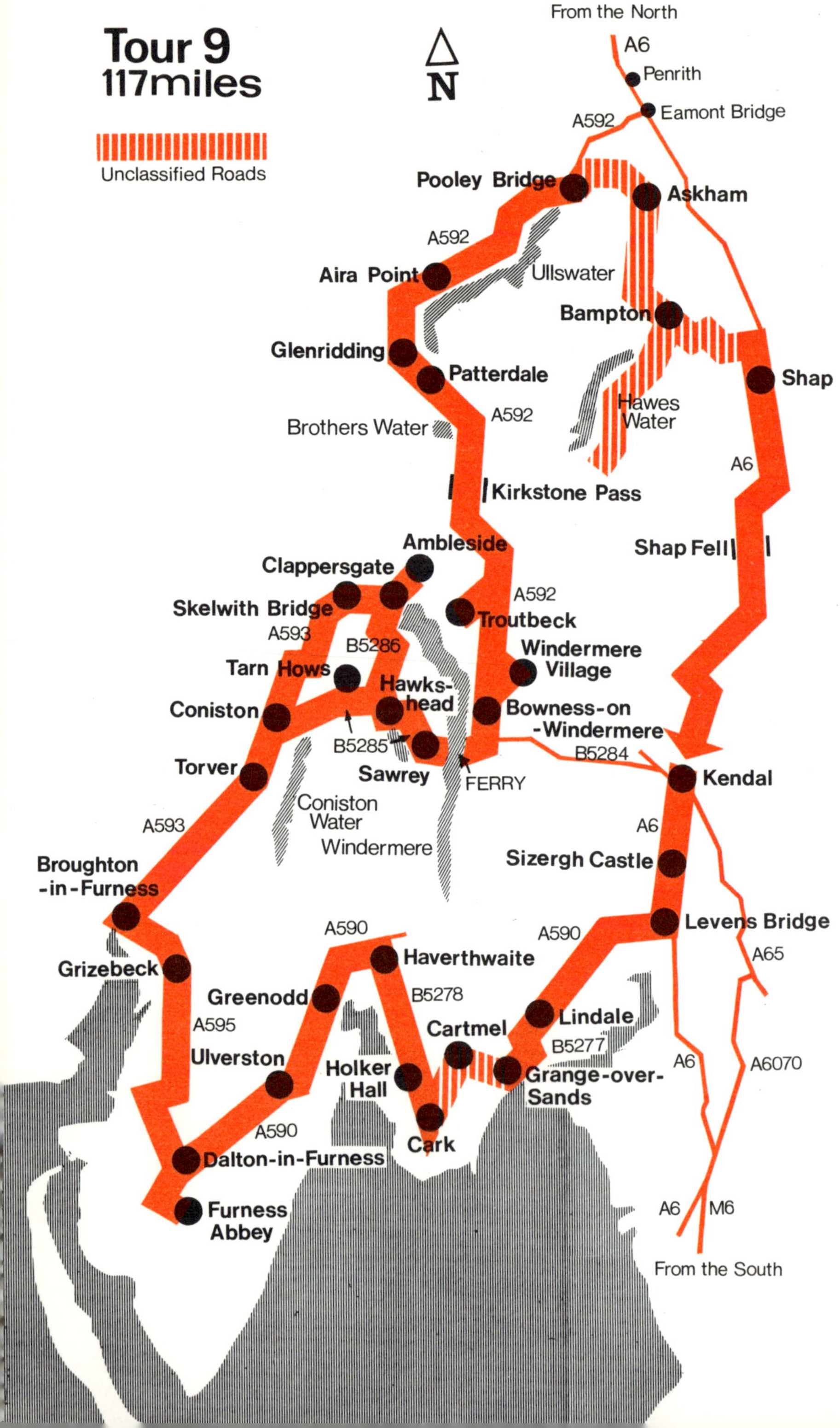
Tour 9
117miles
N
Unclassified Roads
From the North
A6
Penrith
Eamont Bridge
A592
Pooley Bridge
Askham
A592
Aira Point
Ullswater
Bampton
Glenridding
Patterdale
Shap
Brothers Water
A592
Hawes Water
A6
Kirkstone Pass
Ambleside
Shap Fell
Clappersgate
Skelwith Bridge
A592
Troutbeck
A593
B5286
Windermere Village
Tarn Hows
Hawks-head
Coniston
Bowness-on-Windermere
B5285
B5284
Sawrey
FERRY
Torver
Kendal
Coniston Water
Windermere
A593
A6
Sizergh Castle
Broughton-in-Furness
A590
A590
Levens Bridge
Haverthwaite
Grizebeck
A65
Greenodd
B5278
A595
Cartmel
Lindale
B5277
Ulverston
Holker Hall
Grange-over-Sands
A6
A6070
A590
Cark
Dalton-in-Furness
Furness Abbey
A6
M6
From the South

Grange-over-Sands is a quiet seaside resort on the north side of the Kent estuary in Morecambe Bay, across the broad sands of which there are enticing views of the Pennines.

Unclassified road (hilly) inland to Cartmel (2 miles) and thence south-west to Cark (2 miles).

Cartmel is a charming small town with an interesting Priory Church, mainly of the late-12th and 15th centuries, with an unusual diagonal crown to the tower and 15th century oak stalls supporting a richly carved and canopied 17th century screen. In the small square are the 14th century Priory Gatehouse (admission weekdays on application) and the 18th century Market Cross. Cark, which has a 16th century hall, is on the long peninsula stretching between the Kent and Leven estuaries.

B5278 north, passing Holker Hall ($\frac{1}{2}$ mile) and crossing the Leven to Haverthwaite (5 miles); then A590 (coming from Newby Bridge; $2\frac{1}{2}$ miles) to Greenodd ($2\frac{1}{2}$ miles) and thence, west of the Leven estuary, to Ulverston (3 miles).

Holker Hall (admission Easter-September, daily, except Fridays, 10.30 to 6), an early-16th century house much rebuilt and enlarged in the late-19th century, has fine paintings and stands in lovely gardens with a view across the Leven estuary. Greenodd is a village on the Crake (which flows out of Coniston Water) at its junction with the Leven. Ulverston, the 'capital' of the broad promontory of Furness, is an old agricultural town with a large cattle market. On Hoad Hill, above, is a 'lighthouse' memorial to Sir John Barrow, the geographer, who was born here. Swarthmoor Hall, to the south, an Elizabethan and later manor house, was the home of Judge Fell, whose widow married George Fox, founder of the Society of Friends, in 1669.

A590 on to Dalton-in-Furness (5 miles), from which Furness Abbey is 2 miles farther on, to the left of the main road.

Dalton-in-Furness is a market town with a 14th century tower, once the courthouse of the abbots of Furness, in the wide main street. In a secluded valley are the extensive and beautiful red sandstone ruins of Furness Abbey (admission 9.30 to 4, to 5.30, or to 7, May-September; Sundays from 2), mainly of the 12th and 15th centuries, but with graceful 13th century claustral buildings and a 14th century infirmary chapel with two early effigies of knights.

A595 north to Dalton, east of the Duddon estuary, to Grizebeck ($7\frac{1}{2}$ miles) and thence Broughton-in-Furness (3 miles).

Broughton-in-Furness is a small market town on a ridge east of the Duddon's mouth. From Duddon Bridge, 1 mile farther on (by A595), an unclassified road ascends the beautiful Duddon Valley, described in detail in a fine series of sonnets by Wordsworth, to Cockley Beck Farm, at its head (see Tour 10).

A593 across the Furness peninsula to Torver ($6\frac{1}{2}$ miles).

Torver is a small village west of Coniston Water and at the south foot of the Coniston Old Man (2635 feet), the highest of the Furness Fells, of which it commands a splendid view.

A593 to Coniston (3 miles).

Coniston is an unspoilt village ½ mile from the head of Coniston Water, a lake 5¼ miles long with steep, charmingly wooded shores. In the churchyard is buried John Ruskin, who died in 1900 at Brantwood, a house on the other side of the lake (now a conference centre of the Council of Nature) which contains paintings and personal relics. In the village is the Ruskin Museum (admission daily, 10 to 6), which has local material of interest, as well as manuscripts and drawings by Ruskin, minerals gathered by him and further relics. B5285, rounding the head of the lake and leading direct to Hawkshead (see below), passes a road ascending to Tarn Hows, a delectable small lake (very popular in summer), from the high ground near which a superb view opens of Coniston Water and its enclosing fells.

A593 on from Coniston through Yewdale and thence over the shoulder of High Arnside to Skelwith Bridge (5 miles); then right, beyond the Brathay, to Clappersgate (1½ miles), from which Ambleside is 1 mile farther on.

High Yewdale is a farm beyond which a path on the right climbs through Tom Gill for Tarn Hows (see above), ½ mile from the road. From the top of the Oxenfell Pass (526 feet), fine views open of the Helvellyn range ahead and of the Langdale Pikes. Skelwith Bridge is an attractive hamlet on the road to Great Langdale (Tour 10), while Clappersgate is a colourful hamlet farther downstream, below the rugged slopes of Loughrigg Fell.

B5286, crossing the Brathay and rounding Pull Wyke (1 mile), a bay of Windermere, to Hawkshead Hall (2 miles).

Wray Castle, approached by a road on the left, beyond Pull Wyke, is a castellated mansion of the mid-19th century (now a school for Merchant Navy cadets) in beautiful public grounds on the west shore of Windermere. The Court House (admission usually on application) at Hawkshead Hall is in a 15th century gatehouse.

B5285 on to Hawkshead (½ mile).

Hawkshead is an enchanting old village, an intricate network of tiny squares and alleys connected by narrow passages and archways under the houses. William Wordsworth is said to have lodged at Ann Tyson's Cottage, in a lane near Red Lion Square, when he was a pupil at the old Grammar School (at the south end), founded in 1585 by Archbishop Sandys of York. The interesting church, on a knoll close by, is mainly of the 15th-16th centuries and has notable monuments.

B5285 on, along the east shore of Esthwaite Water, to the hamlets of Near Sawrey (2½ miles) and Far Sawrey (½ mile), and thence to Ferry Nab (1 mile) for the car ferry to Bowness-on-Windermere.

Esthwaite Water, 1½ miles long, is one of the quieter and less dramatic of the lakes, separated from Windermere by the wooded and bracken-covered Claife Heights. At Near Sawrey is the small 17th century house of Hill Top (admission daily, Spring Bank Holiday-September, 10.30 to 12.30 and 2 to 5.45; from Easter and in October, weekdays only, 10.30 to 12.30), the home of Beatrix Potter, writer and illustrator of delightful children's stories. From Ferry Nab the car ferry plies regularly each day across a narrow reach of Windermere.

B5284 on from the ferry terminus, then A592 (left) to Bowness-on-Windermere (1 mile).

Bowness is a small town and a very popular summer resort on the east shore of Windermere, with slate-built houses in its narrow and irregular streets, which cluster on the steep north side of a bay. The 15th century Parish Church of Windermere here has 13th-15th century stained glass that includes the arms (the stars and stripes) of the Washington family. From the bay (over-popular in the season), where the steamers from Waterhead (Ambleside) and Lake Side (Newby Bridge) call, a footpath rounds the headland to the south, affording charming views of the wooded islands in the lake and the imposing fells round its head.

A592 north, with enticing glimpses of the lake, then across the Windermere-Ambleside road (Tour 8) and ascending into the Troutbeck Valley for Troutbeck Church (4 miles), before climbing steadily to the summit of the Kirkstone Pass (4 miles).

Troutbeck Church, restored in 1879, has some 17th-18th century woodwork and a window by the Pre-Raphaelite school. The village of Troutbeck (Tour 8) runs along the hillside to the west. The solitary inn at the top of the Kirkstone Pass (1489 feet) is the fifth highest licensed house in England and commands a wild mountain view.

A592 on, descending steeply to Brothers Water (3½ miles) and thence through the dale to Patterdale (2 miles).

Brothers Water is a small lake near the foot of the beautiful Dove-dale, with its fine upstanding crags. Patterdale is a village in the charming dale of the same name, about ½ mile above the head of Ullswater and near the entrance to Grisedale, which penetrates deep into the heart of the Helvellyn range.

A592 on to Glenridding (1 mile), then along the north shore of Ullswater to Aira Point (2½ miles) and on to Pooley Bridge (5½ miles).

Glenridding, the terminus of the motor-yacht service from Pooley Bridge, is a village near the head of Ullswater, the second in size among the English lakes (7½ miles long) and the grandest in scenery (see also Tour 8, page 50). Pooley Bridge is a pleasant village on the River Eamont at its emergence from the lake.

A592 on for 1 mile, then unclassified road (right) to Askham (2½ miles more).

Askham, on a slope above the Lowther, is a delightful village with old whitewashed cottages lining a long irregular green, shaded by sycamores. Near the foot is the 14th-18th century Hall, in attractive gardens, and on the other side of the valley is Lowther Park, one of the largest and most beautiful parks in England, though the early-19th century Castle has been a dismantled shell since 1957. The church, partly of the 12th and 13th centuries, contains numerous monuments of the Lowther family, Earls of Lonsdale.

Unclassified road up the west side of the Lowther valley to Bampton (4 miles) and thence, crossing the river, to Shap (4 miles).

Bampton. From here a road runs south for 2 miles to the dam of Hawes Water, a reservoir 4¼ miles long, created in 1937 for the water-supply of Manchester. The road continues along the forest-clad south shore, passing the Haweswater Hotel, to the head of the reservoir, which is enclosed by a splendid mountain group that includes the long High Street range (2718 feet). Shap is a granite-quarrying village affording fine views of High Street and Saddleback. Shap Abbey (admission 9.30 to 4, to 5.30, or to 7, in May-September; Sundays from 2), in the valley to the west, has 13th century remains and a large 16th century tower.

A6 (very busy in summer) south over the Shap Fells (1397 feet), descending thence at length to Kendal (15 miles).

10. The Lake District, including Windermere and the Western Dales

This tour includes the lesser-known western part of the Lake District. It takes in nine of the lakes, among them the remote Wastwater and Ennerdale Water, as well as the fine old towns of Kendal, Cockermouth (the birthplace of Wordsworth), Keswick and Ambleside, the fascinating villages of Hawkshead and Grasmere, and the valleys of Great and Little Langdale, the head of the Duddon valley, and the green Eskdale, on the west side. Also to be seen are the Roman fort on the Hardknott Pass and the Viking cross at Gosforth, near the west coast; but perhaps the most enchanting aspects of these Lakeland tours are the wonderful and constantly-changing views of the mountains themselves.

Kendal is described in Tour 9 (page 51).

From Kendal by Stricklandgate, Windermere Road and A591 for 1½ miles, then by B5284 (left) through Crook (2½ miles), crossing A5074 and A592 before reaching Bowness Ferry (4½ miles).

Windermere. This road, a quiet approach to the Lake District, affords enticing glimpses of the lake as it descends. Bowness (see Tour 9) is less than 1 mile to the right on A5074. Windermere (see also Tour 8) is the largest lake in England, 10½ miles long, though nowhere more than 1¼ miles wide. Its name, of Norse origin, signifies the Lake of Vinand, not the 'winding lake'. (As the suffix 'mere', incidentally, means 'lake', the term Lake Windermere, often met with, is an unnecessary duplication.) The shores of the lake are thickly and charmingly wooded; the fells in the neighbourhood, if not particularly high, are everywhere rocky and colourful, and the head of the lake is enclosed by a girdle of imposing mountains. A car ferry plies regularly each day across the lake to Ferry Nab (nearly ½ mile).

B5285 from Ferry Nab to the hamlets of Far Sawrey (1 mile) and Near Sawrey (½ mile).

Near Sawrey. Here is the small 17th century house of Hill Top (admission Spring Bank Holiday-September, 10.30 to 12.30 and 2 to 5.45; from Easter and in October, weekdays only, 10.30 to 12.30), the home of Beatrix Potter, writer and illustrator of delightful children's stories. Esthwaite Water, 1½ miles long, is one of the quieter and less dramatic of the lakes, separated from Windermere by the wooded and bracken-covered Claife Heights.

B5285 along the east shore of Esthwaite Water, to Hawkshead (2½ miles).

Hawkshead is an enchanting old village, an intricate network of tiny squares and alleys connected by narrow passages and archways under the houses. The interesting church, on a knoll at the south end, is mainly of the 15th-16th centuries and has notable monuments. William Wordsworth was a pupil at the old Grammar

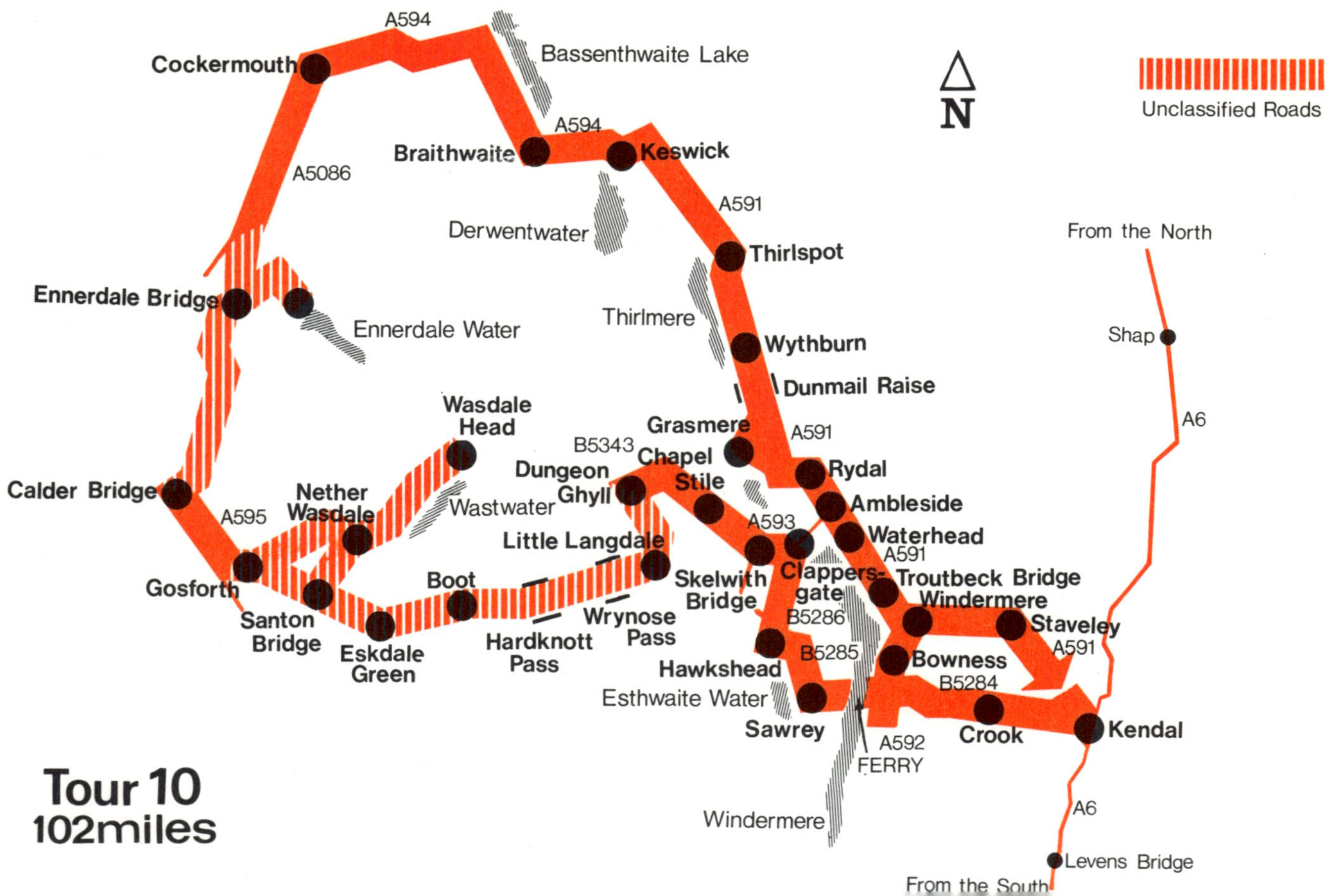

Tour 10
102miles

School, close by, founded in 1585 by Archbishop Sandys of York, and he is said to have lodged at Ann Tyson's Cottage, in a lane near Red Lion Square.

B5285 on to Hawkshead Hall (½ mile), then B5286 on again, rounding Pull Wyke (2 miles), a bay of Windermere, and crossing the Brathay to Clappersgate (1 mile); then A593 (left) to Skelwith Bridge (1½ miles).

Hawkshead Hall has a Court House (admission usually on application) in a 15th century gatehouse. The road on the right just beyond leads to Wray Castle, a castellated mansion of the mid-19th century (now a school for Merchant Navy cadets), in beautiful public grounds on the west shore of Windermere. Clappersgate is a colourful hamlet below the rugged slopes of Loughrigg Fell, and 1 mile south-west of Ambleside (by A593). Skelwith Bridge is an attractive hamlet farther upstream, near the waterfall of Skelwith Force, enclosed by charming woods.

B5343 north of the Brathay and past the small lake of Elterwater to Elterwater village (1½ miles) and thence to Chapel Stile (½ mile), then into Great Langdale for the Old Dungeon Ghyll Hotel (3 miles).

Elterwater, reed-fringed, is one of the least interesting of the lakes, but its shores afford a fine view of the Langdale Pikes. From Chapel Stile, a quarrying village with the parish church of Langdale, the road ascends Great Langdale, one of the very finest of the Lakeland valleys, with a wonderful view of the precipitous crags of the Langdale Pikes, rising dramatically above the valley floor, and of Bowfell and other hills around the valley head. The road passes the New Dungeon Ghyll Hotel, with the kennels of the Windermere Harriers, and ends at the Old Dungeon Ghyll Hotel, a noted resort of rock-climbers. Dungeon Gill Force, between the hotels and near the foot of the Pikes, is a waterfall about 65 feet high in a narrow ravine with sheer rock walls.

Unclassified road, steep and narrow, across the saddle between Great and Little Langdale, passing Blea Tarn, to Fell Foot Farm (2 miles), then right, ascending steeply again, to the top of the Wrynose Pass (1½ miles).

The Langdale Pikes. From the saddle (over 750 feet) between the dales, there is an exciting retrospect of these rugged peaks. The road passes Blea Tarn Farm, "the one abode, no more" of Wordsworth's *The Excursion,* before descending to Fell Foot Farm, at the head of Little Langdale, which is more pastoral and less popular than its neighbour. A winding road climbs to the summit of the Wrynose Pass (1281 feet), linking the Bowfell range with the Furness Fells. The Three Shire Stone here marks the meeting-point of Westmorland, Lancashire and Cumberland.

Unclassified road on, following the upper reach of the Duddon, nearly to Cockley Beck Farm (1½ miles), then across the river and ascending to the top of the Hardknott Pass (1 mile).

Cockley Beck is at the head of the beautiful Duddon Valley (see Tour 9). From the top of the Hardknott Pass (1291 feet), wonderful views open of Eskdale and the Scafell group of mountains.

Unclassified road, with many sharp, steep bends (great care required), passing Hardknott Castle and descending to Eskdale, which is followed through Boot (3½ miles) to Eskdale Green (2½ miles).

Hardknott Castle is an interesting Roman fort (Mediobogdum), recently partly reconstructed, which stood on the road from Ambleside to the port of Ravenglass. Eskdale, the upper reaches of which are enclosed by a magnificent semi-circle of mountains that includes Scafell Pike and Bowfell, is one of the few Lakeland valleys without a lake. Dalegarth station, beyond the small village of Boot, is the upper terminus of the narrow-gauge railway that runs past the village of Eskdale Green and through the level Mite valley to Ravenglass, on the estuary of the Esk.

Unclassified road (right) to Santon Bridge (2 miles) and thence to Gosforth (3 miles).

Santon Bridge is a hamlet on the Irt. From it an unclassified hilly road runs north-east towards the secluded hamlet of Nether Wasdale (2 miles) and thence along the shore of Wastwater, the deepest and most austere of the lakes, with magnificent views of the precipitous Wastwater Screes descending to the opposite shore. This road ends at Wasdale Head (5 miles more), a hamlet with a hotel and a tiny church, enclosed by the steep-faced mountains of the Great Gable and Scafell ranges, the wildest scenery in England. Gosforth has a remarkable Viking Cross, probably of the late-10th century, in its churchyard, sculptured with a remarkable combination of Norse saga and Christian lore.

A595 (right) to Calder Bridge (2½ miles), then right by an unclassified road into the Calder valley for ½ mile; then left by a moorland road (hilly in places) to Ennerdale Bridge (6 miles more).

Calder Bridge. The road passes the prominent atomic energy power stations of Calder Hall and Windscale before descending to this small village. Of Calder Abbey, over ½ mile upstream, there survive some 12th-13th century ruins. From the hamlet of Ennerdale Bridge a very narrow and twisting road descends to the Angler's Inn (2 miles) at the foot of Ennerdale Water, a remote lake at the impressive entrance to Ennerdale, a long trench-like valley, now largely afforested, but hemmed in by grand ranges of mountains.

Unclassified road on from Ennerdale Bridge for 3 miles, then A5086 (right) to Cockermouth (7½ miles).

Cockermouth is a stone-built market town at the junction of the Cocker with the Derwent. Wordsworth House (admission Easter-September, Mondays, Wednesdays and Saturdays, 10 to 12 and 2 to 5), in the tree-lined main street, was the birthplace of William Wordsworth (1770) and his sister Dorothy. The 13th-14th century Castle of the Percys, to the east, approached through a gatehouse of about 1400, was 'slighted' by the Parliamentarians in 1648.

A594 (east) to the Pheasant Inn (6 miles), near the foot of Bassenthwaite Lake, and thence along the west shore to Braithwaite (5 miles).

Bassenthwaite Lake, nearly 4 miles long, is the only 'Lake' named as such in the Lake District. The shore road from the charming old Pheasant Inn commands a fine view of Skiddaw and its satellites opposite. Braithwaite, on the right, is a characteristic village at the foot of the Whinlatter Pass (Tour 8).

A594 on to Portinscale (1 mile).

Portinscale is an attractive village near the foot of Derwentwater (see Tour 8). On the left of the road beyond the Derwent is Crosthwaite church, which is mainly of the 14th and 16th centuries and has a monument (with an inscription by Wordsworth) to Robert Southey, whose grave is in the churchyard.

A594 across the Derwent and the Greta to Keswick (1½ miles).

Keswick is an old-world market town about ½ mile from the north end of Derwentwater and at the foot of the steep, smooth slopes of Skiddaw (3053 feet), which shelters it from the north winds. In the congested Market Place is the Continental-like Moot Hall (1813), and to the north, beyond the Greta, is the pleasant Fitz Park, with an interesting Lakeland Museum (admission weekdays, 10 to 8). Near the lower bridge over the Greta are the Pencil Manufactories for which Keswick is noted (with an exhibition room near by), and on the hill above is Greta Hall, where the poets S. T. Coleridge and Robert Southey lived. Enticing views of Derwentwater and the surrounding fells are obtained from the terrace of St. John's Churchyard, from Friar's Crag, a promontory ¾ mile south, beside the lake, and (best of all) from Castle Head, a wooded crag near the Borrowdale road, from which the 'Jaws of Borrowdale' and the Scafell mountains are particularly well seen.

A591 up the Greta valley, then branching right in 1 mile and crossing the ridge of Castlerigg and the valleys of the Naddle Beck and the St. John's Beck to Thirlspot (5 miles); then on, along the east side of Thirlmere, under the steep slopes of Helvellyn, to Wythburn (3½ miles).

Thirlspot is a scattered hamlet near the north end of Thirlmere, a lake that was converted in 1879 into a reservoir for Manchester, which is supplied by an aqueduct nearly 100 miles long. The level was raised 50 feet by a great dam at the north end, crossed by the road connecting the main road with the quieter road on the west shore, but the lake is now enclosed by thick pine plantations, restricting the views. Wythburn is a hamlet with a tiny 17th century church near the south end of the lake.

A591 on, ascending to Dunmail Raise (1 mile) and thence winding down through the Vale of Rothay to Grasmere (3 miles).

Dunmail Raise (782 feet), the head of the pass crossed by the boundary between Cumberland and Westmorland, affords a charming view forward down the vale to Grasmere, with the jagged rocks on Helm Crag to the right. The large cairn near the road is said to mark the grave of Dunmail, the last king of Cumbria, whose defeat in a battle here in 945 brought Cumberland under the rule of Scotland for over a century. Grasmere village, which lies to the right of the main road, is described in Tour 8 (page 47).

A591 on to Town End (½ mile; see Grasmere), then along the lake shores of Grasmere and Rydal Water to Rydal (2 miles) and through the vale of the Rothay to Ambleside (1½ miles).

Rydal and Ambleside are described in Tour 8 (page 47).

A591 on to Waterhead (½ mile; see Ambleside) and along the east shore of Windermere to Low Wood (1 mile), then on to the hamlet of Troutbeck Bridge (2 miles) and across the Bowness-Patterdale road (Tour 9) to Windermere Village (1 mile).

Low Wood, a hotel on the lake shore (favoured by honeymoon couples), commands one of the loveliest views in Lakeland, the fells from the Coniston Old Man to Bowfell and the Langdale Pikes being especially well seen. Windermere Village is described at the beginning of Tour 8 (page 45).

A591 east, away from Windermere, to Staveley (3½ miles) and thence, west of the Kent valley, to Kendal (4½ miles).

Index of Places